The Complete Guide to Mindfulness Series

Mindfulness in a World of Chaos

Mindful Mornings

30 Day Challenge

by

Rachael Thompson

Complete Guide to Mindfulness

Introduction

Mindfulness is an extremely simple concept but one that can be very difficult to implement. It will instantly reduce stress and anxiety, and with habitual practice, will vastly improve quality of life. It is rooted both in social science and spirituality, and research has proven its effectiveness. Its simplicity and power might be the reason it has gained popularity in recent years.

There are a lot of resources available, but many either over-simplify or complicate mindful concepts. This 3-part series aims to demystify mindfulness. You will find practical information and real-life examples. You will also be given simple activities to guide you through your mindfulness journey. Everything in this book can be implemented in your life, no matter your schedule, responsibilities, or circumstance.

To experience optimal results, read through this book slowly and implement each suggested activity. This is a journey, and every journey takes time. Make a commitment to self-improvement, take a little action every day, and see your new life unfold.

Complete Guide to Mindfulness includes:

Book One: Beginner's Guide to Mindfulness in a World of Chaos

By the time you have finished this book you will know: what mindfulness is and how you can apply this knowledge today, quick and simple meditation techniques, common causes of stress and anxiety and how to combat these using mindfulness, techniques to prevent feelings of regret, and an overall plan to begin making changes for a happier life.

Book Two: Mindful Mornings: Daily Reflections and Meditations to Start Your Day Off Right

Mornings are said to be the most powerful part of any day. They represent a fresh start, a new beginning. Devoting just five minutes each morning to reflection and meditation will transform your days and eventually lead to a more blissful life. Carry these reflections and meditations with you through your days and watch your daily experiences transform. Stress will seem far less daunting; you will be able to enjoy each moment and appreciate those around you as your heart fills with love and gratitude. You owe this time to yourself. Transcend any limitations brought about by negative thinking and experience true peace and deep joy.

Book Three: 30 Day Mindfulness Challenge

The challenge is broken into four, weekly sections, with one bonus day to begin the challenge and another to end the challenge. Each week has a different focus to facilitate optimal learning at each stage of mindful skill development.

You will find both basic and advanced mindfulness concepts broken down and will be given simple, concrete action plans to implement each concept in your life. You will find a new activity every day that takes you one step closer to a happy and peaceful life. Activities can help with all facets of life, from relationships to health to problem-solving skills. Begin the challenge and watch your life transform!

Special Offer!!

If you are interested in kicking this process up a notch and seeing even more dramatic results, sign up to enroll in the FREE Video Training:

http://exclusive.mymbse.com/mindset-makeover-webinar-series/

This 90-minute webinar training provides life-changing techniques for retraining your mind quickly and effortlessly. Learn how to develop your perfect set of affirmations, go through a powerful 20-minute guided meditation to develop a subconscious blueprint that will lead to your ideal future, and finally understand what 99% of self-help material gets wrong and how you can finally see results while others remain stuck. Sign up here to enroll for FREE Today.

http://exclusive.mymbse.com/mindset-makeover-webinar-series/.

MINDFULNESS In a World of Chaos

Contents

Mindful Mornings

Contents

Mindful Mornings

Contents

30 Day Mindfullness Challenge

Contents

Mindfulness

The Beginner's Guide to Mindfulness in a World of Chaos

by

Rachael Thompson

Introduction

"I constantly have so much going on that it feels like life just passes me by."

Does this sound familiar? Have you ever gone hours, days or even years feeling as if you are on autopilot? Many go through life without taking the time actually to enjoy it, and before they know it, their children are grown, their vacation is over, and those whom they thought would always be there passed away. We know we should appreciate every moment, yet get lost in routines and constant stressors. We sadly become a bystander in our lives. This book will allow you to take a step back and examine why this is happening in your life as well as give you simple, actionable steps to begin your mindfulness journey and take control of your life.

This book contains proven strategies on how to live in the moment and reduce stress and anxiety both using mediation and without meditation. The goal is to provide more than concepts and ideas but force you to examine critically and take the lead in your life.

Each chapter covers key components of mindfulness, provides examples and gives you steps to apply each lesson. You can implement them all or focus on just one. It's your journey. Good luck!

CONTENTS

Chapter 1:
Mindful or Mind Full?

There is only the present. Take a moment to reflect on this statement. Now before you think this is some "woo-woo" guru talk, let's examine the truth. The past has occurred, but can you do anything to change the past? No, you never can. You can change your future actions based on lessons learned from the past, but the past will remain unchanged. In fact, the past is just a memory. It is just a memory of the last time you remembered it and studies have shown that humans are often pretty bad at accurately recalling past situations in an unbiased manner. If you never think about a past event again, it disappears because the only thing that keeps the past alive is your recollection of it. The future is nothing more than our thoughts and stories predicting what we think will happen. The future only exists in our minds. When the future happens, it is turned into the present. Unfortunately, humans rob themselves of their present moments by polluting them with thoughts of the past and the future. We endure stressful moments, but they pass. They continue to cause us stress as we ruminate about the past or fear the future. If we simply accept the stress in the present moment and let it go, the amount of stress we all experience will drastically decrease. Humans are doing themselves a great disservice and depriving themselves of the only resource they can never get back, their time. This is where mindfulness comes in.

There has been a lot of talk about mindfulness. Anyone who has taken a yoga class probably heard the instructor speak on it. Self-help material has referred to it for years in one sense or another. The adult coloring book trend has made mindfulness a common term, yet many are still unsure what it truly means. So what is all the buzz about this modern day buzz word? Mindfulness had been a practice rooted in Buddhism as well as a technique used in the counseling field to help those dealing with anxiety, mood and personality disorders much before it became a household phrase. Techniques have been backed by empirical evidence showing its effectiveness in the management of emotions. Does this mean you have to be a yogi, a spiritualist or need to seek counseling to grasp and practice this concept? The goal of this book is to prove otherwise. Anyone, with any amount of time in their day, with any amount of knowledge on this subject, can begin to implement and reap the benefits of this practice.

Mindfulness is essentially the practice of being fully present in your life. This means being mindful of surroundings, other people as well as one's thoughts, feelings, and behaviors. Mindfulness is when you pet your dog and simply feel what the fur feels like to touch without any other thought. It is listening to another's story without placing any of your thoughts or judgments on it and without thinking what you will say next. It is eating a meal and tasting all of the flavors, feeling the textures of the food, and hearing the sounds it makes when you chew and swallow it. It is feeling the breeze on your face, the sun on your shoulders, and hearing birds chirping while you take a walk. Mindful observations help those live in the present moment and take things for exactly what they are without attaching any of one's thoughts to it.

Mindfulness alleviates stress, fear, anxiety, anger, resentment, and guilt and replaces these feelings with peace and contentment. It forces one to live only in that very moment, to become curious about behaviors without labeling them, and prevents people from merely floating from day to day to become the leader of their lives.

Action Steps: For the next 24 hours observe how mindful you are throughout the course of the day. Do not do anything to change your thoughts and behaviors but become an observer of yourself as you walk through life. Take note of your thoughts throughout the day and how much time you spend thinking versus being present in the moment. Also, pay attention to certain situations that bring up positive and negative emotions. You likely will be able to discover patterns in your thought process and behaviors. There will be time to change behaviors in the future, but one must develop a self-awareness to even recognize where changes can be made.

Chapter 2:
You don't have to be a Monk to Meditate

Mindfulness means meditating for hours every day and is surely a practice that not many can do, at least correctly, right? It is a common misconception that prevents people from implementing a mindful practice. Later in the book, we will discuss how meditation is not even needed to be mindful, but for this chapter, we will give you actionable steps for meditation if you want to incorporate it.

Mindfulness meditation is the practice of clearing your mind and focusing on nothing but the here and now without judgment or trying to change anything. With the practice of daily meditation, it will be easier to control your stress and anxiety. You would not run a marathon without extensive training first, and mindfulness should be viewed similarly to any other training that helps you achieve the desired result. The more you work on it, the stronger your mindfulness power and endurance becomes. If you wish to develop a mindfulness meditation practice, it is best to start with shorter amounts of time and increase it. It is also best to pick the same time each day that you can commit to setting time aside to meditate. The more you can practice on a regular, consistent basis the better the overall results. Often people pick morning to practice meditation or right before bed.

Action Steps:

1. Find a comfortable place to either lie straight or sit up. (Sometimes sitting can be better as you will not likely fall asleep).

2. Set a timer. When you start out, it is best to keep it around 10 minutes, but you can certainly increase this as you feel fit.

3. Begin to take calm breaths. Pay attention to how your breathing feels going in your nose, down your lungs and back out of your nose. Pay attention to how your chest or stomach rises and falls as your breath. The crucial component is not to try to change your breathing or make any judgments. This is not a deep breathing exercise. Breathe normally and merely focus your attention on your breath and body.

4. Next, do a body scan. Start with the top of your head. How does it feel? What is the temperature? Can you feel your hair off your scalp? Now move down to your face. What do the back of your eyelids look like? How do your nose, lips and chin feel? Continue this process down your entire body until you reach your toes. Pay attention to temperature and feeling. Notice if there is any tension or tightness but do not try to change or fix any sensation. You are simply noticing sensations and moving on.

5. After your body scan, pay attention to noises. First the sounds of your body. Can you hear your breathing? Focus just on that sound. Next, focus on the sounds in that room. What noises can you hear only in this space? Move on then to outside of that room, to the hallway or other areas of your living space. What noises can you hear? Finally, focus your attention past your living space to the outside. Can you hear anything?

6. Finally, pay attention to how it feels to be at that very moment. Let any thought that comes into your mind float out. Do not judge yourself for falling out of a mindfulness state and do not judge any thought that comes into your head. Do not attach any emotion to anything. Simply focus on sensations. A thought is solely a thought that floats in and out when no attention is paid to it.

7. If you find that one technique works best for you then carry out the rest of the meditation using that technique, if not just "be" until your timer rings.

Chapter 3:
Take a Walk. Easy Right?

One of the top strategies for reducing stress and clearing one's mind is taking a walk. Exercise has been shown to help improve both anxiety and depression as well as alleviate overall stress. Many unfortunately do not take full advantage of this simple stress management tool. Have you ever taken a walk to clear your head only to ruminate obsessively over that which is causing you stress? How many times have you gone for a walk and not remembered a single part of it because you were only paying attention to the thoughts in your mind? People often go over past conversations or occurrences they wished would have gone differently. They also will go over possible future situations, how they wish they would go, all the ways they could go wrong and how they will react.

At the end of a thought-filled walk, one may or may not feel better. Getting your body moving can physically reduce built up tension, however, if your thoughts continue to provoke feelings of stress and anxiety the walk did not accomplish its desired purpose. It is a common misconception that one will find the perfect solution if s/he just thinks long enough about the problem. The result is more often high stress with no solution. When one's mind is in such a state, it is clouded by circular thinking patterns that elicit the same negative solutions. When one clears his or her mind that person is more likely to view the problem from a neutral standpoint without negative feelings swaying his or her outlook. Do not take a walk to clear your mind, rather walk with a clear mind.

At this point, you may be thinking "But this is much easier said than done. How do I even do this?" And you are right. Walking with a clear mind is easier to explain than to practice but is just one more component of mindfulness that requires training and it is possible. When one walks in a truly mindful matter, he or she only pays attention to what is apparent in the physical environment. Observe the sights, the sounds, and the feelings all without judgment. Examine the trees, flowers, physical structures, animals, people, etc. without attaching any additional thoughts or feelings to these observations. For example, if you see a flower garden filled with various types of plants and flowers observe the colors, textures, sizes, smells and whatever else is visible in this garden. Do not place a judgment, either positive or negative, on any of these plants. Do not say "That is a pretty flower." or "That plant stinks!" Not judging when practicing mindfulness will help you place fewer judgments in your daily life, on yourself, others, or situations.

Make sure not to be rigid or critical of yourself during these walks. If you stop to talk to someone along the way, do not allow yourself to think about that conversation for one second after it is done. Once that moment has passed, your focus is solely on what is currently happening. Many thoughts will pop into your head during this walk. Your mind will begin to make associations between what you observe and various thoughts and stories. This is natural as it is what your mind has been doing for years thus it will be uncomfortable not making these associations at first. As with any mindful technique, allow these thoughts to pass through without giving them any attention. The more attention you give these thoughts, the more susceptible you become to getting lost in your thinking and forgo mindfulness. If you realize you have allowed your thoughts to take over for a moment, simply return to being mindful. Do not judge yourself in any way. In the beginning, it will be very challenging to be completely mindful for an entire walk, but judgment does nothing besides take you farther away from your end goal.

Action Steps: Take at least a 15-minute mindful walk.

1. First, focus on your bodily sensations. Start with your feet. How do they feel in your shoes? Feel the sensation of your foot pushing against the ground as your walk. Next, move up your leg, starting at the ankle up to your hips. Observe sensations of temperature, any breeze, bodily sensations and feeling of clothing against the areas of your leg. Repeat this process, scanning up your entire body, until you have reached the top of your head.

2. Once you have completed your mindful body scan, shift your attention to sights. Remember only observe but do not place any judgments on what you see. Pay attention to the color, the texture, the size and shape of all you pass. If you find that this becomes a sensory overload, pick one type of sight to pay attention to. For example, first only pay attentions to the trees you pass, next pay attention to the ground, and finally, pay attention to only the houses you pass.

3. The next mindful technique is to pay attention to sounds. Fist pay attention to only the sounds of your body. Can you hear your breathing or your feet walking? Next shift attention to the sounds around you such as cars passing by, children laughing, people talking, dogs barking.

4. As you become more comfortable with this type of walking, feel free to experiment a bit. Pay attention when certain thoughts pop up. Do you have particular triggers along your walk that elicit certain thoughts and emotions? You can use these mindful observations to guide what you will focus your mindfulness on during future walks. For example, you may notice every time your pass another person you automatically judge them and wonder if they will talk to you which leads to a sense of anxiety about how you will respond. The focus of your mindful walks could then be to only observe people but not with any judgments. Don't think "That woman is wearing an ugly green top." but instead "A woman is walking. She is wearing green, V-neck top and black shorts. She has blonde hair." The more you can simply observe people for exactly what they present, the less you will automatically place judgmental thoughts on others.

Chapter 4:
A Tale of Two Days:
Getting out of autopilot

Many think they have to carve out time to meditate to practice mindfulness, which is not true. Mindfulness meditation can be very helpful, especially to those suffering from certain mental health disorders, but you do not have to meditate to practice mindfulness. In this chapter, we will discuss an everyday mindful practice that you can implement now. Let us look at Lynn's case study for an example.

Lynn has been struggling with stress for years now and wishes she could find a way to feel the calm happiness she enjoyed in her younger, carefree years. She is divorced, works full time and is the mother of two school-aged children. Her days consist of driving the children to school, working nine hours, picking her children up from their after school program and driving them to various activities throughout the week. She spends her evenings helping with homework, packing lunches and preparing for the following day. Weekends are spent running errands and getting everything done that she couldn't get to during the week. The only solace she has is every other weekend when her children visit their dad, and she can watch a movie and partake in several glasses of wine. Lynn wakes up every morning with a pit in her stomach thinking about all that she has to fit into the next 18 hours. She is constantly tired, stressed and snaps at her children and co-workers as a result. She is hopeless that she will ever get out of this routine.

Have you ever felt like Lynn? Perhaps you have an entirely different circumstance but have you ever felt as if you do the same things day in and day out without any enjoyment or end in sight? Many go through life in this autopilot state of existence, and it is not that their lives are without joy, but they are not aware enough to enjoy those moments as their thoughts are constantly elsewhere. Being mindful will not change outside factors, and it will not change what you have to do in life, but it can greatly affect your happiness and enjoyment in doing these seemingly mundane or even stress-inducing tasks. Let's see how.

Let us examine what a day may look like if Lynn was practicing mindfulness. She wakes up, lies in bed for a few minutes and enjoys feeling the soft pillow and sheets surrounding her. She does not think about getting up nor all of the things she has to do once she gets up. She merely feels the comfort of her bed during her first waking moments. She then goes to wake her children. Instead of assuming her children will have attitudes and preparing to yell at them on her walk down the hallway, she simply feels the carpet she is walking on and her fuzzy rode against her body. She sits on the bed to wake up her son and caresses his head, feeling his soft hair. He tells her to go away, but she doesn't react to this. She does not place any meaning to his reaction at all. She simply tells him to get up, and she will be back in a few minutes to check on him. On the way to work, Lynn listens to the radio and observes the cars around her. She gets cut off, which would normally put her day off to a bad start, but instead she takes the incident for what it is and continues listening to the radio. At work her boss tells her that she has to have her report to him by the end of today. She does not think about what an unfair jerk he is but starts to work on her report. At lunch, she peacefully walks to get a salad and decides to eat it outside and enjoy the beautiful spring day. Instead of thinking how angry and stressed she is at her boss and that rude, unaware driver that morning she simply feels the warmth of the sun on her face, the slight breeze blowing through her hair and taste of every bite of food she puts in her mouth. Later that day she takes her daughter to gymnastics. Normally she would be mentally running through everything that happened that day while periodically looking at her watch to make sure practice does not go one minute over schedule as she then has to pick her son up from karate. Instead, she watches her daughter finally stick the back handspring she has been working on for months. As she and her children eat dinner after practice, she listens to their stories about their days without any judgment. She does not allow her mind to wonder to how they still need to shower and do homework in the next hour, but simply listens and is present. While she lies down to go to sleep, she again focuses on her soft pillow and the soft noises she hears through her open window. There is no replay of the day or planning for tomorrow, but she is simply present.

Now, which Lynn sounds like they had a better day? The one who is on autopilot or the one who was fully present and able to enjoy each moment. Mindfulness does not change outside situations, but neither does getting upset or stressed. If she had gotten stressed at the morning driver, it would not have changed the fact that he cut her off. If she had gotten mad at her boss, it would not have changed the fact that her report was due and if she was so busy paying attention to her thoughts she might have missed her daughter's big accomplishment.

The story is not meant to simplify being mindful because it is not that simple. However, it is meant to provide several instances where Lynn had a choice, and she chose to take the mindful route. It should not be expected to be able to simply change to be able to live your entire day in a mindful manner, but the more you can practice it in certain situations, the easier it will become.

Action Steps:

Option 1: Pick one area of your life to become more mindful over the next week. This could be during your morning commute, during dinner or your lunch break. Make sure the event is an hour or less, as it is better to start small and grow. During this set period observe sights, sounds, and sensations without attaching any labels. Do not judge anything or anyone, yourself included. When thoughts pop into your head during this time, simply allow them to pass through as a cloud. If you notice you get sucked into your thoughts, simply break this pattern as soon as you recognize it, without judging, and return to the present moment. If you try this and cannot stay mindful for the initial allotted time break, cut this time amount in half. Perhaps only focus on mindfulness for half of your lunch break and slowly increase by a few minutes each day.

Option 2: Pay attention to moments in your day when you can make a choice to either get upset or stressed or to focus only on the present and incorporate mindful techniques. This will require some self-awareness to implement correctly, but if you can notice an event that is sparking negative thoughts and emotions tell yourself "STOP!" and practice mindfulness. For example, if you notice that after a conversation with your partner you feel angry, dedicate the next 15 to 20 minutes to being mindful instead of replaying that conversation in your head. The more you can become aware of triggers for negative thoughts the more chances you have to replace this self-induced stress with mindfulness. You can also use this technique when you find you are missing out on enjoyable experiences. For example, if you notice you tend to think about work during dinner or other family events, stop yourself and focus only on what is happening at that current moment. You will find a greater amount of enjoyment for yourself and others are likely to notice a change as well.

Chapter 5:
Don't Should On Yourself!
The top tool to prevent all regret

Let's examine the following scenario. Frank has been trying very hard lately to control his angry outbursts at home. Many days he notices his improvement when talking to his wife and dealing with his children. This afternoon, however, Frank has a slip-up and screams at his five-year-old for making too much noise when Frank is trying to get work done. His son cries and runs to his room while his wife glares at him and shakes her head in disappointment. Almost instantly Frank feels guilty. He knows that his son was not making much noise and yelling at him was not the fair way to deal with the situation. Now he feels as if all of his work has been erased with one small slip.

This similar situation plays out time and time again with everyone who is working to change or improve an aspect of themselves. Humans are complex and to think that you can switch on a mindful button, and you will be good to go is quite naive.   When these instances occur, we are often very hard on ourselves. Automatic thoughts arise that we "should" have acted differently, "should" have said this, "should not" have done that. Accompanying these thoughts will often be feelings of guilt, anxiety, disappointment and regret. Humans may even use these thoughts to try to feel better about the situation. If you react negatively and feel guilty after it is better than reacting negatively without the feeling of guilt, right? In reality, feeling guilty or disappointed does nothing to change what happened. It may lead to you apologizing but does it help to prevent this situation from reoccurring? It may, but it certainly is not the most effective technique to use.

Instead of "should-ing" yourself, get curious. Think about what led up to that situation. Let's get curious and dive into what lead to Frank's reaction. In Frank's case, he was very stressed out. Why? He was stressed out because he had a lot of work to get done and only a short period to do it.

Frank thought his boss was unfair to assign him this task. Why? This task was not in Frank's job description, but he had to do it because the company did not want to hire another employee. Also, Frank's boss had been leaving early to golf with his buddies each day that week. Thoughts like "How dare he be able to enjoy time off when I cannot spend quality time with my family, but instead have to work" and "I don't get paid enough for this" and "I can barely afford my mortgage while he can afford to golf every day" were continuously running through Frank's head. Frank was, unfortunately, not being mindful of these thoughts. It becomes obvious that the built up feelings of anger and resentment put Frank in a bad mood, and all it took was one minor event to push him over the edge that day. Once he examines this, he can learn to pay attention in the future when he starts having these thoughts. Stopping the problem at the route through mindful curiosity will yield much stronger results than thinking what you should or shouldn't have done in these situations.

Mindfulness is not simple. You will slip up. To be judgmental or critical of yourself is counterintuitive to the process. With time and a lot of practice, it will become easier and more natural.

Chapter 6:
The Major Point to Take Away and Use Every Day

If you are to remember only one concept in this book, let it be that true happiness lies in the present. Your thoughts make your world the way it is. Two people can experience the same situation but have completely different experiences. Let's look at one final example that has nothing to do with mindfulness to drive this point home.

Two men are waiting at the subway station to go to work. They both have huge presentations to give at 9 am and are heading in early to set up before their clients arrive. Murphy's Law takes effect, and the train is running late. Neither man knows when it will arrive, and neither one can do anything about it. The first man gets angrier the longer he waits while the second man remains calm. The first man continuously thinks of the worst case scenario, that the train will not arrive, he will not make it to work and will get fired as a result. The second man knows he can do nothing to control this situation and uses this extra time to prepare mentally for his presentation. Neither man is being mindful, but one just has a more optimistic view which benefits him in this scenario. Most likely the second man instinctively has more optimistic thinking patterns than the first and as a result experiences less stress and anger. Many factors contribute to why these men differ, including the temperament and personality they were born with, the experiences each had in life, the difference in environments, so on. Humans are far too complex to compare, and it would only cause the first man more stress if he compared himself and wished he was more like the other.

So why provide a closing example that has nothing to do with mindfulness? This is to show just how each experience only differs because of the thoughts attached to it. The situation remains unchanged, but the feelings and level of stress one experiences vary drastically depending on what thoughts one places on events. In mindfulness, everyone is on the same playing field. It does not matter how optimistic or pessimistic you are. You can see situations for exactly what they are without the possibility of stress-inducing thoughts taking over.

There are techniques where you replace negative thoughts with neutral or positive ones to reduce negative feelings, but this is different than mindfulness. You do not combat negative thoughts with positive ones; rather you combat them with an active observation of the present. Thus, there is no need to try to convince yourself that your initial thoughts are wrong. In mindfulness there is no wrong or right, there is only the now.

If you feel as if your life is a rollercoaster between high points and low points, mindfulness will transform this to more of a train ride. You'll peacefully ride along, enjoying the sites and not worrying about plummeting down a huge hill once you reached the top. If you feel as if you walk around in a daze without appreciating your days, then mindfulness will be an incredible tool to open your eyes to all that around you. Like any muscle, you have to train it. Like any habit, thinking patterns and focus will be challenging to alter. And like any journey, the result will be worth all the obstacles you must overcome to get to your destination. Get curious. Start small. Do not judge. Work daily.

Final Action Step:

1. Devise your mindfulness plan for the next week.

2. Pick what technique you will use, when and for how long you will implement it and how you will stay on track.

3. You can decide to experiment with each technique throughout the week or focus on growing one technique before trying another.

4. The important part is that you make a plan and hold yourself accountable to sticking to this set plan.

5. View mindfulness as a chance in your day to let go of all negative feelings, not like a chore or obligation. If at any point it becomes overwhelming, scale back. You will likely have to experiment a bit to find what works best for you. Good luck and enjoy your journey!

Conclusion

Thank you again for purchasing The Beginners Guide to Mindfulness in a World of Chaos!

I hope this book helped you understand what mindfulness means and simple ways you can apply it to your life. Book Two of this series will guide you through daily reflections and meditations that lead to a balanced and blissful life.

Mindful Mornings

*Daily Meditations
and
Reflections to Start Your
Day Off Right*

by

Rachael L. Thompson

Introduction

Mornings are said to be the most powerful part of the day. They are a fresh start, a new beginning, the sunrise to limitless possibilities. Most, however, spend their mornings in a stressed, tired, and rushed state. When one begins the day in such a manner, it becomes impossible to regain any sense of peace or happiness as the day progresses. It is time to take control of your mornings. Take a few moments for yourself to reflect and meditate on what truly matters in life. Carry these reflections with you throughout your day and watch as your internal and external worlds shift.

This book provides reflections and activities that will slowly and effectively transform your life. Reflections based in fields of philosophy, psychology, and both Eastern and Western spirituality provide a holistic view of well-being and self-development. Read a new reflection each morning or choose to focus on one category for an extended period, allowing yourself to master the concept. Although the reflections are based in theory, the author provides meditation and reflection activities to incorporate the theories easily into your everyday life. Make the commitment to do so, and watch your life change.

The final part of the book provides ten different meditation guides. These guides provide simple, easy-to-follow steps and can effortlessly be incorporated into every morning. Meditation is a powerful tool that can be used in a variety of ways, such as reducing stress, improving health, reprogramming natural thinking patterns, increasing energy, and expanding consciousness. Use the guides to find a meditation that works best for your goals and try to incorporate it into your daily life.

Contents

Contents

Part I
Reflections and Actions

Chapter 1: A Mindful Morning

"Most humans are never fully present in the now, because unconsciously they believe that the next moment must be more important than this one. But then you miss your whole life, which is never not now. And that's a revelation for some people: to realize your life is only ever now."

~Eckhart Tolle

There is only the present. Take a moment to reflect on this statement. The past has occurred, but can you do anything to change the past? No; you never can. You can change your future actions based on lessons learned from the past, but the past will remain unchanged. In fact, the past is just a memory. Studies have shown humans are often bad at accurately recalling past situations in an unbiased manner. If you never think about a past event again, it disappears because the only thing keeping the past alive is your recollection of it. The future is nothing more than our thoughts predicting what we think will happen. The future only exists in our minds. When the future happens, it is turned into the present. Unfortunately, humans rob themselves of their present moments by polluting them with thoughts of the past and the future. We endure stressful moments, but they pass. They continue to cause us stress as we ruminate about the past or fear the future. If we simply accept the stress in the present moment and let it go, the amount of stress we all experience will drastically decrease. Humans do themselves a great disservice and deprive themselves of the only resource they can never get back, their time. This is where mindfulness comes in.

Take some time now to fully embrace this present moment. Allow any thoughts of the future or past to pass through your mind, like clouds in the sky. Be mindful of the sights, sounds, smells, and bodily sensations. Notice how your mind resists this stillness. It wants to constantly think, but this is your time to just be. Take a few minutes to enjoy this mindful experience now and set an intention to live a mindful day. Try to be as present in each moment as possible throughout the rest of today, especially during any moments of stress or tension.

Chapter 2: Gratitude

"Do not spoil what you have by desiring what you have not; remember that what you now have was once among the things you only hoped for."

~ Epicurus

Gratitude has been called the proven key to happiness. We often take for granted how much we have to be grateful for. Instead, we focus on frustrations, lack, and what we want but do not have in life. Unfortunately, this is the way humans are naturally programmed. The reason you are here right now is because your ancestors survived. They survived by paying attention to negatives. For example, once somebody learned snakes are venomous. Humans remembered this and avoided them, hence we survived. We also have an urge to acquire more, to have better. If we did not, we would still be living in caves and not in high-rises with all the latest technology.

The problem with this mindset is that although it is great for survival, it is terrible in terms of happiness. Our brains were built for survival, not happiness. We naturally remember negatives far longer than positives. It can be changed, but it takes effort. This is where practicing gratitude helps. Research has found practicing gratitude will help you savor positive experiences, leading to the highest amount of enjoyment in life. It can help you develop better problem solving skills without letting obstacles stop you from accomplishing your goals, it can help with social interactions, encourage a willingness to help others, and can prevent negative feelings of jealousy and anger from interfering with your new mindset.

The best part about gratitude is it is very easy to add into your day. You can think of what you are grateful for first thing in the morning or right before you drift off to sleep. You can practice it during your morning and evening commutes. You can practice in solitude or with your partner or children. You can add it in any time you feel down or overwhelmed. This practice will help you get out of a mental rut, learn to focus on positives, and view situations in a more objective manner and the more you practice it, the easier it becomes to savor all of life's blessings.

Take some time now to list three to five things you are grateful for in your life. These can be people, situations, health, abilities, etc. Any time today you feel frustrated, envious, or upset, pause and say three to five things you are grateful for in that moment. There is always something, even if it is as simple as being grateful for the sunshine or the ability to move your limbs. This practice will instantly change your outlook and your mood.

Chapter 3: Stress-Free Day

"The greatest weapon against stress is our ability to choose one thought over another." ~William James

Stressors are inevitable. As much as we would like for life to be easy and free flowing, it is more like the waves of the ocean than a still lake. Like waves in the sea, there are ups and downs. They are as beautiful as they are dangerous. But those who focus solely on the potential dangers of the ocean never get to experience its true beauty. The sea will always have waves, sometimes they are soft and rolling, while other times they are choppy and relentless. Neither state lasts forever. Remember this as you experience stress in your life. When things are good, experience the beauty of that moment without fearing potential future 'danger' or stress. During stressful times, repeat the mantra 'This too shall pass'. No state, neither good nor bad, lasts forever.

Stress often comes from resistance or the need to control situations. Have you ever tried to swim out into a choppy ocean? It is not only difficult but incredibly draining. Resisting stress is like swimming against the current. You will drain all your energy without getting anywhere. The only thing you have control over is your mind. Try not to let stubbornness, resistance, or the need for control cause unnecessary stress. You cannot control the ocean but you can control your actions in relationship to it. Perhaps wait until the next day when the waves have calmed down, find an alternate way to swim, or even sit at the shore while the waves crash against your feet. These alternatives are far easier than fighting a losing battle with the harsh current. Yes, you must change your plans a bit and do a little problem solving, but your body and mind will be much healthier for it.

Think of any current or past stressors that were made more difficult because of resistance. What would it be like if you simply accepted what is and instead of fighting searched for an alternative? Throughout the rest of your day, try to relinquish all control and resistance. Any time you feel stress, stop to ask yourself, "Do I have any control over this right now?" If the answer is yes, then problem solve to overcome it. If the answer is no, focus on what you can control in that moment. What can you do in that moment to reduce your stress? This is a great time to become present and mindful, call a friend, or think about a goal you plan to work on. There is always an alternative.

Chapter 4: Self-Awareness

"What is necessary to change a person is to change his awareness of himself."

~ Abraham Maslow

Self-awareness is typically defined as being conscious of how we act or are perceived by others. This is a part of self-awareness, but not the complete picture. Another component of consciousness is the focus on what is going on within ourselves. We have hundreds of thoughts running through our heads every minute that cause different feelings, bodily sensations, and actions. How aware are you of these thoughts? Have you ever stopped to ask yourself why you think, feel, or act in a certain way? All our actions are made with the intention to make us feel better and these actions can be beneficial or detrimental to ourselves or others, but nonetheless, at the time we act, it is always with the intention of inducing happiness.

If I just have this glass of wine, I will be relaxed. If I help this other person, they will appreciate me and this will make me feel loved. If I say something nasty to my coworker it gives me a sense of control, which makes me feel better about myself.

These thoughts might not be easily apparent without a strong sense of self-awareness, but they are what underlie all actions. Unfortunately, many actions lead to regret, remorse, and stress instead of fixing the underlying issues. By cultivating a strong self-awareness, you can get to the underlying thoughts and discover your true needs. There is a need to relax. Perhaps a glass of wine isn't the answer, but working on stress management in daily life is. You should not have to put yourself out in any way to feel loved. The focus instead should be on unconditional self-love. And if you want to feel better about yourself, putting others down is certainly not the way to do so. The solution would be self-work to cultivate a sense of control without having to put others down to feel this way.

Self-awareness of this nature takes practice. Throughout the day, practice by paying attention to your thoughts and actions and ask yourself what needs you are trying to meet. Next, think of any positive alternate ways to meet these same needs. Question where certain thoughts come from. We all have some limiting or dysfunctional thinking patterns that developed at a young age and no longer serve us. Can you think of any now? Self-awareness will help you uncover any beliefs that no longer benefit you so you can change them. Take special notice of these thoughts as you practice your self-awareness. Over time, self-awareness will enable you to meet your underlying needs in the most positive and effective manner possible.

Chapter 5: Family

"There is no such thing as a 'broken family.' Family is family, and is not determined by marriage certificates, divorce papers, and adoption documents. Families are made in the heart. The only time family becomes null is when those ties in the heart are cut. If you cut those ties, those people are not your family. If you make those ties, those people are your family. And if you hate those ties, those people will still be your family because whatever you hate will always be with you."

~ C. JoyBell C.

Families can be our biggest support system, largest source of stress, greatest source of happiness, and biggest teacher. We all have the ability and inability to choose our families. We have no control over the family we were born into, yet as we grow into adults we take back the control as we pick partners and friends and decide to have children. A common mistake is thinking that because we chose people to be part of our lives, this then gives us control over such individuals. This is the quickest way to disharmony in any relationship. By relinquishing the urge to control relationships, we open ourselves up to harmonious love and limitless growth potential in these relationships.

The understanding of human behavior will be your greatest asset in forming harmonious relationships within your family. As adults, we often harbor resentment for the mistakes of those who raised us. We see our past situations through the narrow vision of our own perspective. This resentment does nothing but eat away at our own peace while interfering with new relationships. By workings to develop an understanding for those who raised us, we are better able to free ourselves from the negativity we continue to hold on to. We can forgive ourselves and others, knowing we are all human and by nature make mistakes.

This same understanding will also help foster healthy current relationships with family members. Being able to understand and appreciate others for who they are and not who you think they should be will free both you and your family from unnecessary pressure. Encouraging others to become their greatest selves is best done with an understanding of who the person really is. Once you have this understanding, you can easily appreciate all the wonderful, unique characteristics of the family member and communicate in a way that resonates with his or her distinctive personality.

***Disclaimer: This reflection is a suggestion and not intended as a therapeutic practice. If you have experienced significant trauma, please seek the help of a professional.*

Do you continue to hold any negative emotions towards family members? What will it take for you to release this negativity? Take a moment to put yourself in their shoes. People in pain pass on pain to others. They do this for reasons that can be hard to understand for others and even for themselves. Try to empathize with those who caused you pain. Imagine them as little children, who themselves were in pain with little control over their situation. It often makes it easier to picture those who hurt us in their innocent form, as everyone was an innocent baby at one point. As you picture them, express your sympathy for their story. Tell them you let go of any pain they caused and free yourself from the hold of the negativity.

Is there any current family relationship causing you stress, anger, or frustration? What is the source of the negativity? Take a moment and imagine this relationship from the other member's perspective. Empathize with any of their experiences and negative emotions. Is there any part of the relationship you can relinquish control of and allow them to be the people they genuinely are? How do you think this will free you from negative emotions and encourage a better relationship?

Chapter 6: Appreciation

"The roots of all goodness lie in the soil of appreciation for goodness."

~Dalai Lama

When was the last time you felt and/or expressed appreciation? When was the last time you felt appreciated by others? We all want to be appreciated, yet many of us lack the clarity of mind to really appreciate our circumstances, especially once circumstances become routine. A mother who makes dinner for her family six nights a week, often puts a lot of effort into this task, between meal planning, grocery shopping, and preparing the meal. Yet the family eats the food with little appreciation. Her children only act appreciative the one night a week they go to a restaurant to eat. Now take a parent who does not cook and the family eats take-out every week. If that parent cooked a meal, the family would be more likely to appreciate it. This is simply because human beings become habituated to situations. If a child or spouse has a home-cooked meal every night, they learn to expect it and once this habituation occurs, it takes effort to appreciate the event.

If you are lucky enough to have a car, I am sure you rarely think of what a luxury this is. If this car was taken away and you had to rely on other forms of transportation, you would miss the ease of being able to quickly drive wherever you wanted to go. The reason you do not appreciate your car each time you drive it is because it has become a part of your daily routine. You expect it will reliably get you from A to B and you never stop to think of what a privilege it is. Everyone takes people, material goods and various conveniences for granted. It is not something to feel guilty about, merely something to be cognizant of.

Often, when we think of appreciation, we focus on how we wish others would appreciate us more. It would be nice if everyone appreciated everything we do for them, but without awareness and effort, many are not able to do this. We can have conversations with the people we love about lacking appreciation, and this may work depending on the person, but the only person we have guaranteed control over is ourselves. Instead of wishing others showed you more appreciation, turn your focus towards your appreciation for them.

Are there things in your life you have become used to and thus lack awareness and appreciation for? Perhaps something a friend, spouse, parent, or sibling does? Take a moment to think of something that if it was not there, you would miss. It can be as simple as your children telling you they love you before bed or your coworker bringing you coffee each morning. The more habituated we become to an event, the less likely we are to feel and express genuine appreciation.

This acknowledgment and expression of appreciation will make you feel good and help you value the people in your life. Making this a habit will become contagious. It may take some time, but eventually others in your life will pick up on this appreciation.

Take some time to write the top 3-5 things you appreciate but have neglected to acknowledge or express. Plan how you will let others know your appreciation for them and their actions. Throughout the rest of today, make note of anything in your life you can be appreciative of. Mentally note the event, allow yourself to feel the appreciation, and if appropriate, express that appreciation to the other person. Give yourself this same gift. Say thank you for everything you do. Appreciate that you get out of bed and provide for yourself and/or your family (whether through work or through actions). Appreciate any time you take for self-care (exercise, reading, taking a bath). And appreciate all you do to make others' lives a little better. You may not get appreciation from your children for cooking dinner, but this does not mean you cannot appreciate yourself for taking the time and effort to make sure your family has a nutritious meal.

Chapter 7: Problem-Solving

"No problem can be solved from the same level of consciousness that created it."

~Albert Einstein

The key to success is creativity, and problem-solving is nothing more than a creative approach to a problem. Those with successful relationships didn't just stumble upon marital bliss. Rather, the success of their relationship can be attributed to their ability to problem-solve. Those with successful businesses and careers likely experienced a plethora of challenges and overcame those challenges to reach the successful position they currently hold.

There are multiple ways people handle problems. Some ignore problems. Some avoid any situation that could cause problems. Some become defeated and give up when faced with problems. Some become defensive and look for a scapegoat when problems arise. And some tackle the problems head-on and overcome them.

How do you approach problem-solving? And how has this approach led to different outcomes during your life? Could your life be made better with a different approach to problem solving? Do you view problems as a personal weakness? Do you try to hide or cover-up your problems from others? Do you constantly ruminate over problems, allowing them to interfere with other areas of your life? Do you suffer from indecisiveness or the curse of perfectionism?

Changing your mindset about problems changes the way you approach them. Problems are bound to arise. Your personality type, experiences and how you were raised all affect the way you perceive challenges and how you attempt to overcome them. Think now of a recent challenge you have faced or one you are currently facing. Is there a way you can think about it differently? Without blame, guilt, anger, or resentment try to think of an alternative way to view this specific problem. Practicing different ways to view situations will help facilitate and improve your problem-solving skills. Everything is a challenge you can overcome. It may not be quick and it may not be easy, but it can be done.

During your day, simply pay attention to your initial reaction to problems. This can be as small as your local coffee house being out of your favorite blend or more significant work or family related problems. Notice your initial reaction. Are you quick to anger, get frustrated or feel overwhelmed? Do you want to solve the problem as quickly and painlessly as possible, not matter what? Or do you easily go into a creative problem-solving mode. Knowing your natural tendencies is a starting point to change. If you catch yourself before you allow your natural tendencies to take you down a rabbit hole of frustration, you can consciously change your mindset and try to think of new, creative ways to solve each problem. And if it is not a big problem, remind yourself it is not worth too much energy and can be solved quickly by making a simple decision and moving on.

Chapter 8: Relationships

"The meeting of two personalities is like the contact of two chemical substances: if there is any reaction, both are transformed."

~Carl Jung

The word relationship is very broad. You can have a relationship with coworkers, friends, spouses, family, and acquaintances that vary drastically from person to person. Think now of relationships that bring you the most joy. What about this relationship causes you happiness? Take a moment to contemplate the dynamics of these relationships and be grateful for them.

Now think of relationships that cause you any feelings of negativity or parts of relationships with others that cause you negativity. Where exactly does this negativity come from? We all play a part in relationships, so for now focus on the role you play in this negativity. Often our minds hold on strongly to negative emotions surrounding relationships. We hold on to guilt, resentment, anger, jealousy, and bitterness, which clouds our perceptions of others and ourselves. Are there any relationships you still hold negative emotions around? How do you think this affects your role in the relationship and your state of mind daily?

We too often allow adverse past experiences to fill us with negativity. We carry a dark cloud of emotion that interferes with how we interact with others and with how we view ourselves. It is time to free yourself of this negativity.

For today, try to be present and mindful in each interaction you have. If you have any immediate negative reactions, ask yourself what is causing this. If interactions bring up past hurt, make a note of it but try not to allow this past hurt to overwhelm you with negativity. Also, be mindful of pleasant interactions you have with people. If your coworker makes you laugh or your spouse gives you a compliment, take just a moment to express internal gratitude and appreciation for that relationship.

Chapter 9: Communication

*"To effectively communicate, we must realize that we are all differ-
ent in the way we perceive the world and use this understanding as a
guide to our communication with others."*

~Tony Robbins

Communication is an essential part of life. Being able to communicate
effectively is incredibly important yet often we fail to do it well. Com-
munication is much more than talking. It involves tone of voice, body
language, using relatable language, and most important active listening.
It only takes one misspoken word, one misinterpreted body signal or a
careless statement to turn a normal communication into a miscommuni-
cation. One of the biggest sources of contention in relationships is a lack
of effective communication.

Have you ever had something you said misinterpreted and taken the
wrong way? Have you ever tried to express yourself and ended up feeling
unheard and misunderstood? Have you ever misunderstood what anoth-
er was saying and immediately jumped to a conclusion?

Our brains are interesting beasts. If we get incomplete data from our out-
side world (i.e. from our communications), our minds automatically fill
in the missing pieces. Read the following sentence and fill in the blanks:

Susie dropped her books in the hall and bent down to pick them up.

If you were asked to describe the situation in more detail, what would you
say? Perhaps Susie was a student, of a certain age, and was walking in the
school hallways when she dropped her books? If you read the sentence,

there is no indication Susie is any age or that she is even at a school. Susie could be a mother who dropped books she was carrying in the hallway of her house. She could be a publisher who dropped books she was carrying in the hallway of her office building. There are countless possibilities, but without complete information being available, your mind drew its own conclusion based on your reality. If your mother was a high school teacher, whose name was Susie, you might infer the Susie in this story was a teacher who dropped her books in the halls of a high school.

If our minds do this with a simple sentence, think of how often this same phenomenon occurs in conversations with others. Our internal state and natural tendencies drastically affects our interpretations during conversations. With a little observation and introspection, you may be able to pick up on your own conversational patterns. Do you have a general outlook on life that effects how you interpret information? Do you automatically jump to negative conclusions? Do you want to give everyone the benefit of the doubt? Do you impose your own values and view on others in a judgmental manner? Are you always nervous someone will be displeased or angry with you? Are you quick to become defensive? Your natural inclination towards others and towards communication will affect how you fill in the blanks when information is missing.

The simple solution is to work on listening before responding. Listen fully to what others are saying without jumping to any mental conclusions and without thinking of what you will say next. A technique that counselors use to make sure they understand clients is called active listening. This is when you engage in the listening process and reflect to the person what you heard. Once you reflect what you heard, the other individual will either agree or correct you on what they meant. This is a hard skill to master, mainly because our brains are used to working a mile a minute. How often have you zoned out in the middle of a conversation? How often has a person you were talking to asked a question about something you just covered? It is because our brains have a hard time staying focused. We naturally want to skip over parts of a conversation and fill in the blanks. With actively listening, you are completely mindful and engaged, making this zoning out process almost impossible and drastically increasing the quality of all communication.

In all your conversations today, aim to engage in active listening. Be fully present during each conversation. Paraphrase what the other person said to make sure you heard it correctly and be mindful of anytime you are filling in the blanks or jumping to conclusions. Others will notice. People rarely feel genuinely listened to, and your act will help others to feel appreciated and ideally more inclined to reciprocate when it is your time to talk.

Chapter 10: Energize

"The energy of the mind is the essence of life."

~Aristotle

Energy is the essence of everything. All living beings and nonliving objects are made of matter and all matter is energy. One of the biggest sources of our own energy comes from our thoughts. Humans waste a lot of energy thinking. Take for example a day spent using a lot of mental energy. By the end of a day like this, you feel as, if not more, drained than if you had spent the day exerting physical energy.

Energy also acts as a magnet. Have you ever been in the presence of someone who is genuinely upbeat and optimistic? Being around this type of energy tends to elevate our own energy levels. Have you ever laid on the couch all day, feeling guilty for doing so, but unable to find the energy to get up? In these situations, your energy is vibrating at such a low level it takes twice the amount of willpower to even move. If you forced yourself to hop up and march in place for a few minutes, this energy would drastically shift, yet finding the willpower to do so at times feels nearly impossible.

Spiritual texts from various faiths have referred to thinking and beliefs as a form of manifestation. Mathew 25:29 states *"For whoever has will be given more, and they will have an abundance. Whoever does not have, even what they have will be taken from them."* This simply describes the magnetism of lack thinking and energy versus abundance thinking and energy. Those with a poverty mindset will do nothing more than attract more of the same into their lives.

A quote by spiritual leader and author of *Autobiography of a Yogi*, Paramahansa Yogananda, explains energy as *"To understand karma, you must realize thoughts are things. The very universe…is composed not of matter but of consciousness. Matter responds, far more than most people realize, to the power of thought. For will power directs energy, and energy in turn acts upon matter. Matter, indeed, is energy."*

What type of energy magnet are you? What results have you seen from putting out different types of energy? Know that working to change your energy will change the outcome of your life, and if you believe in past and present life karma, it will work to change that as well. Willpower is essential for any energetic shift. Your mind may try to talk you out of working to shift your energy so it can avoid having to exert this willpower. Think of your life as laying on the couch, knowing you should get up while continuing to talk yourself out of doing so. Will yourself to hop up and begin moving. This simple exertion of power will begin a flow that shifts your energy, your thoughts, and your actions.

In every action and thought today, ask yourself what type of energy you are putting out. If the thought or action does not act as a magnet for the energy you want to attract, then work to change it. For example, if you have a negative thought about a coworker, this will temporarily fill you with negative energy. Do you want to attract negative energy to yourself? If not, then work to change your thoughts and shift into a more positive, magnetic energy. This is not to say you have a Pollyanna, blindly optimistic, approach to life. Rather, do not allow you mind to ruminate on the negative. See the situation for what it is and use your mental energy to problem-solve rather than wasting it on things you have no control over.

Chapter 11: Power of Your Thoughts

"You are today where your thoughts have brought you; you will be tomorrow where your thoughts take you."

~James Allen

As explained in the previous chapter, thoughts are nothing more than energy. A simple thought controls your feelings, actions, and bodily sensations. If you watch a scary movie and a thought pops into your head that you may become the next victim of the slasher serial killer from the movie, this thought will be accompanied by feelings and bodily sensations of fear. Your heart rate may quicken, you might begin to feel tension or signs of anxiety. This thought could also lead to actions, perhaps triple checking you locked all doors before you head to bed for the night. If you instead chose to watch a romance movie, a whole new slew of thoughts and feelings could have followed.

This example illustrates how something as simple as watching a movie can create thoughts that lead to various outcomes. On a larger scale, thoughts can determine who you talk to, if you apply for a new job, how you interact with others, the view you have of yourself, and every action you take throughout your day. Knowing this power, one must be very mindful of the thoughts they hold as truth.

Thoughts pop up automatically and we have little control over them. However, we have control over if we believe them and if we allow them to dictate our actions. Examining your own automatic thinking patterns gives you invaluable insight into your behaviors and decisions. Is there something you are afraid of? Is there something you want to do but haven't found the bravery to try yet? What thoughts do you hold about yourself and others? These are all deep questions that can take a while to contemplate, but the more you practice paying attention to your own thoughts, the more you will be able to direct yourself towards the life you want.

Throughout the day, simply be a mindful observer of your own thoughts. Anytime you have a negative emotion, such as fear, anxiety, frustration, or anger, make a mental note of what thoughts led to that emotion. If you can, replace any irrational thoughts with ones that lead to a more positive and peaceful internal state. Overtime, you may be able to discover patterns in your thinking that led you away from becoming your greatest version and accomplishing the goals you want to achieve. Once you discover these patterns, you can work to change and replace them with thought patterns that propel you forward instead of holding you back.

Chapter 12: Goals

"You cannot change your destination overnight, but you can change your direction overnight."

~ Jim Rohn

Goals are often viewed in a very strategic, surface level manner. One may set a goal to lose weight by summer or to earn X amount of money over the next year. Execution of these types of goals takes planning and commitment and it is easy to calculate if you reached the goal or not. Either you lost the number of pounds you wanted or you didn't. You earned your intended salary or you didn't. This type of goal-setting framework can be helpful, but the rigidity of it can also hold you back.

There is a far less common, yet far less rigid way to view and work towards goals. This involves viewing the underlying needs and desires behind each surface level goal. This type of goal setting can be encouraging when thinking of life goals as it does not restrict one to a set of inflexible criteria that needs to be met for the goal to be accomplished. This explanation may seem a bit esoteric at first, but once the concept is grasped it can be eye-opening.

An example is if a woman had the life goal of being a wife and a mother. The rigid form of this goal would require her to find a mate and reproduce with him. What if she reached her mid-thirties without finding that special someone? Would she frantically marry the next man who came around while she was still in her healthy child-bearing years? Now what happens if this mate started abusing her? Would she still want to have children with him because that was her goal? This may be a bit of a dark example, but the point is life does not always cooperate with the goals we set and often people choose a less happy life merely for the sake of accomplishing their goals.

If the woman in this example examined her underlying reasons for being a wife and a mother, she may discover she has a need to provide and care for others. She has a lot of love she wants to share and a lot of lessons she wants to teach. These goals can be accomplished in a variety of ways. Yes, she can still become a wife and mother, but she could also become a teacher, a caretaker, and share her love with thousands of children in need across the world. With this mindset, she can be a mother, without a husband. She can be a wonderful wife even if she is unable to bare children. And she can meet her needs even if she never becomes the wife and mother she yearns to become.

Think now of your life goals. How rigid are they? Have you ever settled to accomplish a goal in a specific time frame? Take some time to write each major life goal you have and make a list of the underlying needs you are trying to meet with this goal. If you have a goal of earning more money, think of what this wealth would mean to you. More freedom, security, a sense of power? Whatever your goals are, think of alternative ways to meet the same underlying needs. This does not mean you should give up working towards your current goals. It will simply give you a more expansive way of viewing them as well as give you comfort knowing that even if your life does not pan out exactly as you have planned, there are various ways to accomplish your desires.

Chapter 13: Self-Love

"Love yourself first and everything else falls into line. You really have to love yourself to get anything done in this world."

~Lucille Ball

There is one constant, unconditional love, and that is self-love. If you practice a spiritual belief, this love comes from the divine love of the Universe, Source, God, Divine Mother, whatever name you want to use, as the love of the divine is constant and unwavering and there is divinity in each one of us. If you do not have a belief in a high-power, you are still able to foster a sense of love for the essence of who you are at your core. The key to loving oneself is to let go of perfectionism and accept oneself as a fallible, imperfect human deserving of love.

Envision yourself as a small child. A child who just made a silly mistake. Would you yell at that child, telling them they should have known better while fostering a feeling of hatred for that child because of the mistake? Sounds a bit extreme, right? Yet this is often how we treat our adult selves.

We do not deserve love unless others love us. We do not deserve love unless we are perfect. We do not deserve love unless (fill in the black).

Take the word "deserve" out of your vocabulary right now. You are loved because you are a beautiful, living creature. The world can be cruel, but often we are crueler to ourselves than any stranger or loved one can be to us. In the end, all we have is ourselves. Yes, we can be surrounded by friends, family, and loving pets, but when all of this is gone, what is left? If you depend on others, accomplishments, or material goods to feel loved then you will never be able to truly appreciate anything in your life.

One must love him or herself before he or she can fully love others. If one is filled with negativity, due to self-hatred, it is hard to see the positive aspects in others and situations. This negativity can cause one to unfairly judge, not be able to enjoy happy moments, and constantly fear something bad is going to happen. If you do not think you deserve happiness, there will be a constant fear and subconscious sabotage that will cause these happy moments to be short-lived. Life is too short for such a mental and emotional state. It is time to take back control of your happiness and foster the unconditional, self-love you deserve.

Take a moment now to think of what type of thoughts you typically think about yourself. Do you have regrets, guilt, or any other negative emotion you are holding on to? Do you constantly sabotage yourself or do you think you are undeserving of happiness? If you have time now, write down all the negative thoughts and emotions you are holding onto. Throughout the rest of today, pay attention to any negative thoughts about yourself that arise. Try to add in a practice of self-love anytime these negative thoughts pop up. Mentally state or say "I release this negative thought now and choose to love myself. I am deserving of love" Overtime, you will be able to let go of habitual thoughts and feelings that bring you down. Once you eliminate these, your entire being will feel much lighter and you will notice how easily you can love others and enjoy life's moments.

Chapter 14: Change

"It is not the strongest of the species that survive, nor the most intelligent, but the one most responsive to change."

~ Charles Darwin

The only aspect of life that remains constant is change. It is inevitable. In some moments, we may pray for change; in others we may fear it. But it comes no matter what our feelings are surrounding it.

What is your relationship to change? Are you change-seeker, constantly looking for the next thing to make life exciting? Or are you a change-fearer, wishing life would always stay the same and resisting the possibility of change at all costs? Many exhibit both types of thinking. When life is hard, redundant, or dull, we may daydream about how welcome a change would be. When life is going great, perhaps a new relationship, birth of a child, moving into a dream house, we want to stay in these moments forever.

The only problem change causes is a result from our own perceptions, thoughts and behaviors surrounding it. If we daydream or constantly search for the next best thing, we train our minds to never be happy and content in the present. When we suffer great pain, knowing change will come eventually, helps to give us hope. When we are content, change makes us fearful. What many neglect to recognize is change is always neutral, and it is our thoughts that causes the positive or negative emotions associated with it.

Having constant thoughts of: *I want more. This doesn't make me happy enough. There must be something better out there.* Causes feelings of restlessness about one's situation.

Having constant thoughts of: *This too shall pass. It must get better. It always gets easier over time.* Provides us with feelings of comfort.

And having thoughts of: *This is too perfect to last. I wish this would go on forever. I never want this to change.* Causes feelings of fear.

Patanjali Yoga Sutra 1.12 states – *These thought fluctuations are mastered through the practice of nonattachment.*

The less you are attached to change, the less it will affect your life. If you are in an uncomfortable state, practice being in that state. In the practice of yoga, many yogis will hold poses and just be in the feelings. If you hold a pose for several minutes, your body may feel fatigued, your mind wants to focus on every slight discomfort, and you start to tremble a bit. In this moment, you can focus on how badly you want to move, or you can be still and breathe through the moment. This is a practice you can use in simple, everyday situations. If you are stuck in a traffic jam, you can focus on how badly you want to get out of the jam and how frustrated you are or you can reassure yourself the jam will not last forever and just be in that moment. The traffic jam or the yoga pose's duration will not be changed if you allow yourself to be in the moment, but your experience in those situations will drastically change if you free yourself from your attachment to them.

This same practice can be applied to happy situations. If you are attached to staying in that moment forever, your mind will distract you from being fully present. Be grateful for happy moments and remind yourself to be fully present without any attachment to how long the moments last.

Today is the perfect day to re-evaluate your attachment to change. In each moment, remind yourself change is inevitable. Enjoy each pleasant moment fully. If you get an hour for your lunch break, enjoy each minute instead of dreading going back to work. If there are slight in-conveniences, remember these will shortly pass. Anytime today that a situation brings up emotions of fear, anxiety, frustration, or anger, say to yourself "I am willing to release any attachment I have to this situa-tion." Allow yourself to sit in discomfort, knowing change is inevitable. And allow yourself to enjoy bliss, also knowing change is inevitable.

Chapter 15: Freedom from Fear

"I must not fear.
Fear is the mind-killer.
Fear is the little-death that brings total obliteration.
I will face my fear.
I will permit it to pass over me and through me.
And when it has gone past I will turn the inner eye to see its path
Where the fear has gone there will be nothing.
Only I will remain."

~Frank Herber

Fear comes from a lack of trust. Lack of trust in ourselves, others, and the universe. We fear car accidents because we do not trust other drives. We fear spiders because we do not trust they will not bite us. We fear job interviews because we do not trust ourselves to do well. We fear the future because we do not trust the universe or a divine power to provide for us. How would your fears transform if you developed a strong sense of trust in everything?

Fear is only made worse by our need for control. In extreme cases, fear leads to anxiety disorders, such as Obsessive-Compulsive Disorder and Phobias. Individuals suffering from these disorders will plan their lives around controlling this fear. An individual may think s/he needs to check all appliances 20 times before leaving the house to prevent any possibility of a fire. Another person may avoid traveling in fear of a plane crash.

Extreme cases of fear can drastically hinder one's life, but even small, seemingly 'normal' fears can have a negative impact. Fear may prevent you from networking or taking advantage of opportunities. It may prevent you from talking to someone you have a crush on. It may cause unnecessary worry about loved ones. It can consume your thoughts, taking away from everyday enjoyment. How has fear impacted your life and well-being?

Think of your biggest fears as well as little worries that consistently cause anxiety or nervousness. How much do you allow fear to interfere with your life? How much of the fear comes from lack of trust? How much comes from an attempt to control your situation?

Throughout the day, be aware of thoughts that arouse fear. Each time you notice a fearful thought, affirm "I trust in myself and the universe (may replace 'universe' with the word you use to describe a higher power: God, Source, The Divine) to act always for highest and best good. I relinquish any need for control and release all worry now."

Chapter 16: Self vs. Others

"Love a person the way they need to be loved, not the way you want to love. It's not about you. Love is selfless, not selfish."

~Tony Gaskins

A common struggle for those on a path of self or spiritual development is how much effort to devote to oneself versus helping others. It seems admirable to live life devoted towards the well-being of others, and it is, but only if it is done for the right reasons. Few people are truly altruistic in every intention and often a longing to help others comes from a selfish or self-serving need. A person with an extreme fear of rejection may become a people-pleaser to avoid any possible feelings of rejection. A mother who does everything for her family may do so in an attempt to avoid negative feelings from her painful childhood. It is not bad to try to live selflessly, but one must work through any self-serving needs to do this in a balanced, and unbiased manner.

On the other end of the spectrum, are those who have a difficult time emerging from self-involvement. It is nothing to be ashamed of, but rather something to become aware of and work to transcend. Often fear, anxiety, frustration and disappointment stem from high self-concern. A fear of public speaking stems from an individual being overly sensitive to his or her own experience during the event. If s/he shifted this focus to the experience of the audience, the fear would diminish. A couple who was out-bid trying to purchase their dream home can transcend their disappointment by focusing on being happy for those who will be living in the house.

A true sense of selflessness is freeing. It is also very difficult to master. The first step in this process is to become introspective. Discover all underlying desires that cause self-serving actions and then work through any past trauma or experiences to free yourself from these needs. After introspection, begin to act in ways that counteract these natural tendencies. For example, if you fear confrontation, look for harmless ways you can confront others. Perhaps debate a friend on which restaurant is the best in town. If you tend to be self-concerned, engage in a conversation where you focus solely on the other person. The counteractions will begin to neutralize undesirable behaviors and bring you a step closer to balance.

Where do you fall on this spectrum? Do you have people-pleasing tendencies? If so, ponder what needs you are trying to meet for yourself. Next think of ways you can work to overcome and counteract them. Do you tend to be highly self-concerned? How does this negatively impact your life? Think of how you can change some of your habits or thinking patterns to develop a perception that expands past yourself.

Chapter 17: Judgement

"Our judgments judge us, and nothing reveals us, exposes our weaknesses, more ingeniously than the attitude of pronouncing upon our fellows."

~Paul Valery

Judgement is one of the most destructive, least productive habits, yet few live a life free from judgmental thoughts. Judgement and peace are incompatible. One can never experience genuine peace while holding onto judgements. Judgement becomes so habituated in us that we naturally do it, without even realizing it. We judge ourselves as a form of punishment for not being the perfect beings we believe we should be and we judge others to make ourselves feel better. This phenomenon is illustrated by the vast increase of reality TV shows, tabloids, and obsession with certain celebrity lifestyles. This is all a judging game. Either we look up to others and judge ourselves in comparison to them or we judge others to make ourselves feel better.

I may not be happy with my body, but at least I am not obsessed with plastic surgery like her. (Insert false sense of pride.) *I wish I could have a relationship like those people I follow on Instagram.* (Insert jealously over a fake reality of someone else's life.)

People who are truly happy with themselves do not feel the urge to judge. The first step on this path to freedom is to accept there is nothing perfect in the universe. Even the beauties of nature have their flaws, and every single human being is flawed. It is the nature of humanity. Accept yourself, right now, as you are and accept others in the same way. We all came into this world with different personalities, had various experiences that shaped us and continue to face challenges. It is unfair to ever judge anyone, especially when using surface level characteristics as a platform for your judgement. Make a vow to yourself today to let judgements go.

The second step on your path, will be to stop all comparison. Do no compare yourself to the 20-year old at the gym and do not compare yourself to the 20-year-old version of you. When you are truly focused on a path of self-development you will be improving every single day. Each day focused on self-love, nurturing positive relationships, and freeing yourself from judgement is one step closer to genuine bliss. Shift all focus to how you are bettering yourself for your own well-being so you can be a positive influence in your world. This focus will provide encouragement and increase willpower to continue your journey.

Have you ever been around someone who seems genuinely happy and exudes positivity? When you are around such people, it seems impossible to feel negative emotions. Aim to be that person. Do you have people in your life you can truly be yourself around without fear of judgment? Aim to be that person to everyone you come across. This does not mean you allow people to walk all over you or engage in activities that can be harmful. You can still give advice and guidance, but this guidance will come from a place of pure love instead of judgement.

The more you can break away from the negative energy that comes out of judgement, the higher your own energy will grow. Self-realized spiritual teacher, Swami Kryananda, stated that thoughts are attracted to us based on our level of consciousness. Raise your level of consciousness, and raise the vibration of your thoughts. Judgement represents a low vibration, while thoughts of peace and love are high vibration thoughts. Work to raise your consciousness, and eliminate those thoughts that bring you and others around you down.

Pay attention to any time you judge yourself or others today. Stop yourself and say "I fully accept myself and others without judgement." Next ask yourself if these thoughts are bringing your closer or further away from your goals. Do not hold onto any thought that does not raise your vibration. Also, pay attention to any people or experiences that cause judgmental thoughts and if you can, work to eliminate these from your life. For example, if you notice certain music, television shows, social media or acquaintances increase judgmental thoughts, think of how you can change your lifestyle to eliminate these. This may mean choosing more uplifting forms of entertainment or eliminating social media from your life. The changes may seem hard, but they are the easiest way to reduce negativity and raise your own vibration.

Chapter 18: Forgiveness

"Inner peace can be reached only when we practice forgiveness."
~ Gerald G. Jampolsky

You should never forgive.

Wait, what??

This statement likely contradicts everything you have heard about working through challenging situations and obtaining peace, but in reality, it is one of the only ways to achieve peace with difficult situations and people. Forgiveness is actually anti-peace because it puts you, the forgiver, in a state of power. A highly freeing approach is acceptance and understanding.

If a child makes a mistake, you are able to understand what made the child act in a certain way. Perhaps they fell victim to peer pressure or an urge for instant gratification. Perhaps they were trying to problem-solve and used the only tools they knew how at that time. Perhaps they only focused on the present moment instead of long-term consequences. There are countless reasons why children make mistakes, and often adults can see the error in the child's thinking and behaving to correct it. Adults also make mistakes for similar reasons, but other adults have a more difficult time accepting and understanding these mishaps. *You should have known better* is a common excuse to become upset with others for making mistakes.

The truth is both children and adults act in ways they think will bring them happiness at that time. Perhaps a person knew better when acting selfishly, but in that moment, for many reasons, he or she thought those actions would bring happiness. A mother who constantly lashes out at her children is likely trying to get rid of a stressor to make a situation better. A teenager who decides to binge drink at a party likely does so with hope s/he will be approved by his or her peers, which will bring happiness. This understanding of others does not mean their actions were "right". Both the mother and the teenage in these situations could have made decisions that were less harmful to themselves and others and would have brought more happiness, but in those moments these alternatives were not considered with an appropriate, unclouded mindset.

Being harmed by the actions of others can be extremely painful, but the only aspect of the situation in your control is your mindset around it. Forgiveness may make the other person feel better, if they want to be forgiven, but true understanding and acceptance will make you feel better. Once you accept and understand you can properly label the action. If a person apologizes, try not to simply say "It's okay" but try to understand what motivated them to act in a way that caused you pain. This understanding fosters growth within yourself and in your relationships. We are all fallible. We often must make mistakes to learn and grow. It is just a part of life. A recognition and acceptance of this is a far more powerful tool than simple forgiveness.

The same understanding needs also to be applied to oneself. We often want to continuously punish ourselves for mistakes we made in the past. Remember, you were doing what you thought would cause happiness at the time, with what you knew how to do in the state of consciousness you had. If you lived a portion of your life in a lower state of consciousness, it is likely you made many mistakes. Looking back now, it may be hard to understand but always try to remember your state at the time. Anytime thoughts of anger or guilt arise, be willing to let them go. You have learned, grown, and continue to grow and you no longer need to punish yourself for the actions of your past.

Think if you are still holding on to any anger or resentment for mistakes you made or mistakes others made. What will it take for you to understand and accept each situation? This process can take years to fully complete depending on the situations, but holding on to any negative feelings only damages your mind and your body. If this is not a process you have worked on before, start with something small. Perhaps a co-worker ate your lunch last week. How will you be able to understand and accept the situation without holding on to any negative emotions? Remember you are doing this for yourself and not as pass for anyone else.

Chapter 19: Health & Wellness

"Your body holds deep wisdom. Trust in it. Learn from it. Nourish it. Watch your life transform and be healthy."

~Bella Bleue

Health is a broad term that encompasses all aspects of one's being. There is physical health, emotional health, spiritual health, and mental health. Often, we can be very focused and devoted to one area while neglecting some of the others, however, all the areas are interconnected. Exercise and healthy eating have been shown to have an impact on mental health disorders, including anxiety and depression. Mental health in turn, plays a role in a person's physical health, often making it difficult to eat right and engage in physical activity. The tendency to focus on one area can be more detrimental than one expects. A marathon runner can have a heart attack by neglecting to engage in stress-management. A spiritually healthy person may focus solely on spiritual devotion, while neglecting their physical well-being, making it increasingly harder to participate in their spiritual practices.

There are multiple wellness models that state anywhere between three to nine pillars of wellness. Common ones include: emotional, career/ job, social, spiritual, physical (including both activity and diet), financial, intellectual, creative, and environmental. To achieve optimal wellness, it helps to dissect your own well-being to discover what areas to focus on. These areas can build on one another and once you have developed healthy habits and found success in one area, you are free to focus on the next. Do not worry that you may unintentionally neglect one area of wellness by choosing to focus on the next. If you are already in the habit of eating well and exercising, you will not begin to neglect these if you decide to focus on creative wellness. You will find that the more areas of health and wellness you can master, the easier it will become to add in new ones.

Examine the following 9 pillars of wellness as they apply to your own life. Rate each one on a scale of 1-10. 1 being an area you completely neglect and/or are very unhappy with and 10 representing an area in which you have found success. Once you have rated each area, choose which part of wellness you would like to focus on over the next month and devise a plan to do so.

9 Pillars of Wellness:

(Derived from The Ohio State University Wellness Center)

Emotional Wellness

The emotionally well person can identify, express, and manage the entire range of feelings and would consider seeking assistance to address areas of concern.

Career Wellness

The professionally well person engages in work to gain personal satisfaction and enrichment, consistent with values, goals, and lifestyle.

Social Wellness

The socially well person has a network of support based on interdependence, mutual trust, respect and has developed a sensitivity and awareness towards the feelings of others.

Spiritual Wellness

The spiritually well person seeks harmony and balance by openly exploring the depth of human purpose, meaning, and connection through dialogue and self-reflection.

Physical Wellness

The physically well person gets an adequate amount of sleep, eats a balanced and nutritious diet, engages in exercise for 150 minutes per week, attends regular medical check-ups, and practices safe and healthy sexual relations.

Financial Wellness

The financially well person is fully aware of financial state and budgets, saves, and manages finances to achieve realistic goals.

Intellectual Wellness

The intellectually well person values lifelong learning and seeks to foster critical thinking, develop moral reasoning, expand worldviews, and engage in education for the pursuit of knowledge.

Creative Wellness

The creatively well person values and actively participates in a diverse range of arts and cultural experiences to understand and appreciate the surrounding world.

Environmental Wellness

The environmentally well person recognizes the responsibility to preserve, protect and improve the environment and appreciates the interconnectedness of nature and the individual.

Chapter 20: Life Purpose

"The purpose of life is to live it, to taste experience to the utmost, to reach out eagerly and without fear for newer and richer experience."

~Eleanor Roosevelt

Pondering the purpose of life can seem daunting, confusing, and fill one with doubts and fears about 'getting it wrong'. It is a subject that can be addressed from multiple angles, spiritual, occupational, familial, etc. There have been entire books written on the subject from numerous viewpoints, but for this chapter, let's summarize it in just one sentence...

A life purpose is to live only for yourself and only help others in the process.

Sounds selfish and contradictory, right? Let's examine a bit further.

"To live only for yourself" simply means live the life that is true to who you are, deep down inside, before your parents, friends, teachers, and society conditioned you to be the person they thought you should be. There is no perfect life or perfect way to live life. Those who feel unfulfilled have often devoted their lives and defined their purpose by the measures of society and not their true values. The only way to discover your life purpose is to get rid of all the conditioning, forgo societal norms, stop caring about judgement from others, and go within yourself to discover who you really are and what you really want for your life. And the most important step is to act on it! Know you can accomplish your purpose and take steps every day to live a life that is true to you.

Now, the second part of the sentence "and only help others" means a true life purpose is accomplished without hurting anyone. You shouldn't have to scam, compete, lie, and cheat to get ahead if you are in alignment with your true purpose. Yes, you will come across people who test you. If you are starting a business or applying for a new job you will have competitors. But remember, this is your life purpose and nobody else's. Challenging people help you grow. Competitors in business or the workplace only show there is a need for the work you want to do. Only you will fulfill your purpose in a particular way and the right people will be drawn to you for it. You may unintentionally 'hurt' others who disagree with your choices. Perhaps your parents are upset that you will never use that law degree or your friends get mad you can no longer meet them for weekly beers because you are busy traveling. Often the people who get 'hurt' by you bettering yourself only need to work through something on their own. Ideally, your life will help inspire those who initially disagreed or didn't understand what you were doing.

So live for yourself, help others in the process and you are bound to wake up fulfilled and fall asleep accomplished most days of your life.

Reflect now on the extent to which you are living in such a manner. If you are not living for yourself, who are you living for? Your spouse, children, parents, society? If you could do anything without the worry of judgement or disappointment, what would you do? Do you focus on others more than yourself? Do you tend to compete with or use others for personal gain? And finally, what is one step you could do today that would lead you one step closer to living your life purpose?

Chapter 21: Confidence

"If you have no confidence in self, you are twice defeated in the race of life."

~Marcus Garvey

Confidence is a huge component of overall well-being. Being confident will help with career growth, relationships, self-image and self-esteem, interactions with others, and various other aspects of life. Often people can be very confident in one area, perhaps video game skills, yet insecure in another, maybe social interactions. To be fully confident and comfortable with yourself in all situations is truly invaluable.

[Note: Because this area is complex and a common struggle for many, this chapter is structured a bit differently. It is designed as a guide rather than a reflection with focus on action as well as observation of one's thoughts. There is also an example of a social confidence action plan to illustrate appropriate execution of the action steps.]

An unfortunate misconception comes from a confusion between confidence and arrogance or cockiness. You see the muscle head strutting his stuff around the gym, and wish you could be that confident. Or you hear a coworker bragging about yet another project he has been asked to work on and you think if you had his level of confidence, you would be able to achieve the career success you crave. These examples of bragging and high self-involvement do anything but demonstrate true confidence. Let's break down the difference between true confidence and the confidence cover-up and then discuss how to reach the real confidence we all desire.

Confidence: Comes from a true, internal sense of self. You do not need to prove anything to anyone because you know exactly who you are and aren't constantly searching for others' approval. Many quiet and humble people are the most confident. They recognize and appreciate their own unique traits and honor those in others. Life is not a competition for them. These people are the most comfortable for anyone to be around as they are neither awkward nor constantly trying to prove themselves. They talk easily as well as listen fully to others without thinking what they will say next.

Cockiness & Arrogance: This stems from the ego and constantly needing to feed it. It's a facade. Such people need to put on the appearance of confidence to feel confident. They need to talk about themselves as a way of proving to themselves and trying to convince others of how great they are. Deep down, they are extremely insecure. They rely on outside reactions and opinions and on their own extreme defense mechanisms to make them feel good.

Now that we have differentiated between true confidence and the confidence façade, let's examine **4 steps to overcome self-doubt and increase confidence**.

Step 1: Pay attention to the story in your head.

What do you tell yourself about your abilities in particular areas? What automatic thoughts come into your head when you think about your ability and confidence in areas that cause nervousness and self-doubt?

Step 2: Understand yourself...and I mean really understand yourself. Looking back into your past, was there a time you were more confident? What has changed since then? Experiences reinforce confidence or lack of confidence. Negative experiences or a lack of experience both can contribute to low confidence. Knowing what fuels a lack of confidence will help you problem-solve ways to overcome it.

Step 3: Combat Negative Thoughts & Change Your Subconscious Thinking Patterns.

Confidence comes from the thoughts you have surrounding your ability in a particular area. Once you examine any negative thoughts you hold you can combat them with more positive or rational thoughts. For example, if asked to speak in front of a large crowd you may have immediate thoughts of embarrassment. By simply reframing and replacing these thoughts with ones that support how well you will present the topic, you can reduce anxiety and increase confidence.

Step 4: Practice.

Often the reason one's confidence remains low is simply because s/he is too fearful to try. The more you practice anything, the easier it gets. Nobody got in a car the first time, truly confident they would know how to drive, but with practice, the confidence grew and we drive every day without thinking about it. The same goes for any skill you are trying to master. The more you try, the more comfortable you become and the more confidence you develop.

Think about an area of confidence you want to improve. Using the 4-Step Technique, devise a plan to help improve confidence in that area. (See example on the next page for more information and an illustration of this process.)

Example: 4-Step Technique to Improve Social Confidence:

Step 1: Pay attention to the story in your head.

When you get an invitation for a social gathering, what thoughts immediately pop into your head? Likely thoughts that lead to some fear or anxiety about going. Possibly you start to doubt if people will like you. Or maybe you fear you won't fit in or will embarrass yourself. These thoughts might then be followed by thoughts of how you are shy or how you wish you had more confidence and finally, how you will not even bother going, telling yourself it's not worth it. The more you avoid these situations, the bigger the story in your head becomes about how terrible they might be.

Step 2: Understand yourself...and I mean really understand yourself.

You were not always this way. Babies and small children act exactly how they want without any fear or embarrassment. There is no such thing as low self-esteem or confidence in an infant's world.

So, what changes over time??

As we grow, our minds begin to develop based on our experiences, what we observe, and what we are taught. Most of our subconscious is formed before the age of 2 so much of this learning occurs by simply observing our parents and other people in our lives. As we learn and develop, certain behaviors and personality traits form. They are then reinforced over time and as we reach adulthood, we have developed ingrained characteristics. Characteristics, such as low self-esteem and self-doubt form part of our self-concept. A truth you hold about yourself, on a subconscious and conscious level, is you have low self-esteem or perhaps you are shy/nervous/anxious.

Know this is NOT THE ACTUAL TRUTH but something you unintentionally picked up along the way and it CAN BE CHANGED!

Once we develop these traits, we will mostly pay attention to situations and experiences that support these. (It is a psychological concept called the confirmation bias). For example, if you have low self-esteem you will automatically focus on experiences that made you feel nervous, shy, and bad about yourself. Perhaps the last time you told a joke to a group of people, they smiled instead of laughed. You will hyper-focus on the lack of laughter and even think about it far after it happens. This in turn, will prevent you from telling a joke in the future, in fear that others will not think it is funny and you will be judged for telling it. You also will easily dismiss any situations you felt or came off as confident. In this same example, you can look at it as you made people smile. How great! But nope, those smiles are not good enough. A socially confident person would take that as confirmation that others liked the joke but a non-confident person will take it as indication of judgement or failure.

In this step, start to dig deep and try to remember where this all started, experiences that reinforced it along the way, and continue to pay attention to the thoughts you have surrounding situations that make you feel less confident. Once you begin to catch these, you will then be able to change them.

Step 3: Combat Negative Thoughts & Change Your Subconscious Thinking Patterns.

Once you get in the habit of observing your negative thinking and recognize it as learned thinking patterns (not the truth), begin to replace these thoughts with self-confident ones. For example, the next time you are invited out and a negative thought pops up, replace it with "I will confidently interact with others." It might help to develop a list of positive thoughts you can use to replace common negative thoughts you experience. I also highly suggest using affirmations or meditations to re-program your mind for success.

Step 4: Practice.

Set a goal for yourself to do at least one thing every month (or every week if you want to kick it up a notch) that forces you to socially interact. There are meetup groups or social outings with friends or coworkers that will provide plenty of opportunities for practice. Know it may be uncomfortable, but you are not going to die and neither is anybody else. Social anxiety and fear is extremely common, so remember you will not be the only one who is feeling a little shy or uncomfortable. Sometimes even telling other people what you are trying to do will help break the ice. Nobody is perfect and others admire people who can openly talk about this instead of trying to put on some facade. The more you practice, the easier it will become. Avoiding these situations, although it seems easier, will only make this much worse as the years go on.

Chapter 22: Peace

"If the problem can be solved why worry? If the problem cannot be solved worrying will do you no good."

~Shantideva (8th Century Buddhist Scholar)

Peace comes from freedom from attachment. It comes from raising awareness beyond one's limited perspective and observing life from an expansive view. Peace is incompatible with worry, fear, anxiety and even excitement. A common misconception is peace is something to be found, but your search will be eternal if you do not first find peace within yourself.

The following quote from Spiritual Leader, Dr. Wayne Dyer, explains exactly where peace is found:

"Peace isn't something you ultimately receive when you slow down the pace of your life. Peace is what you're capable of being and bringing to every encounter and event in the waking moments of your life. Being peaceful is an inner attitude you can enjoy when you've learned to silence your incessant inner dialogue. Being peaceful isn't dependent on what your surroundings look like. It seldom has anything to do with what the people around you think, say, or do. A noiseless environment isn't a requirement."

If peace if your goal, turn your search inward. Be the peace you want to see in the world. Be the peace in your home, at your job, and in your relationships. Observe how the people and circumstances change in response. The more you practice this internal peace, the less reactive you become in life. Allow your higher self to take over. Forgo attachment to experiences in life. Allow others to be fallible beings without attaching judgement to their actions. When you can do this, you will be free.

Today, focus simply on bringing peace into your world. Remember you are only in control of your own thoughts. Try to be the peace you desire. With each thought and action today, ask yourself "Will this bring me peace?" If the answer is no, choose another thought or action that will.

Chapter 23: Inner Bliss

"Nothing is more important than reconnecting with your bliss. Nothing is as rich. Nothing is more real."

~ Deepak Chopra

When one experiences true inner bliss, there is absolutely nothing that can take it away. Most of us search for small moments of happiness that light a candle in our souls. However, as soon as a gust of wind blows, the candle we tried so hard to light blows out and our search begins again. Attaining everlasting bliss is the lighting of an eternal candle, one that cannot be blown out no matter how strong the wind may become.

To escape the cycle of relighting the fragile candle within us, we must first understand where internal bliss comes from. It does not come from material goods, exciting events, success, wealth, or accomplishments. It instead comes from the recognition, appreciation, and unification with our true selves. This is the part of you that remains constant. The part of you free from the ego. The Sanskrit word used in Hinduism for this is jiva, or immortal essence. This describes your soul, your energy, your everlasting self. The ancient Hindu text, the Bhagavad Gita, describes jiva as unchanging, eternal, infinite, and indestructible. Jiva is not an element of the material world but is of a high spiritual nature.

Recognizing oneself beyond what can be seen or experienced in the physical world is the first step to uniting with the jiva, the infinite self. The ego will block you from doing this. It will try to tell you that you are defined by your job, the car you drive or how many friends you have. The more one identifies with the ego, the further they pull away from inner bliss. The more you can break away from the ego and the attachment you have to it, the closer you will become to attaining a genuine blissful state.

Spiritual terms, such as Enlightenment and Self-Realization, are used to describe this break from the ego, the body, and the material world. (The following descriptions are very brief overviews meant only to share an introduction to these practices. Further study and exploration is needed to embark on the path to inner bliss).

Enlightenment, a term used in Buddhism, is a state of perfect wisdom combined with infinite compassion. Naturally we are drawn to what satisfies the ego, and with years of reinforcement we become solidified in this ego, rather than our true selves. A pattern that destroys inner peace. When one breaks free of this pattern and awakens to the true self, they have reached enlightenment.

There are three goals of the Buddhist path and the three accomplishments that mark the attainment of enlightenment: 1.) follow the Dhamma, to fully know what should be known (specifically know your true self) 2.) abandon what should be abandoned (including all mental states that cause illness and suffering) 3.) develop what should be developed (develop insight-wisdom). These are extremely simple concepts, yet this simplicity should never be confused with the ease in which they can be accomplished. With concentration and devotion to practicing these principles, one embarks on a path leading to inner peace.

A second spiritual state of inner bliss is called Self-Realization, described as freedom from karma, when your kundalini (energy) is raised to the highest vibration, and when your chakras are completely clear and balanced. There are multiple paths to this state, including yoga (in particular Kriya Yoga) and meditation, but they require time and deep commitment to the journey.

An easy way to start is simply affirm the following statement from self-realized master and founder of the Self-Realization Fellowship, Paramahansa Yogananda, every morning:

"I am just coming from the inner perception of my Self. I am not the body. I am invisible. I am Joy. I am Light. I am Wisdom. I am Love. I dwell in the dream body through which I am dreaming this earth life; but I am ever eternal Spirit."

Take this quote with you throughout the day. Anytime you feel unsettled by any circumstance, remind yourself of your true essence. You are not your body. You are not your thoughts. You are not your belongings. You are not the opinions of others. Your essence is love. It is joy. It is wisdom.

Reflect on how much your ego determines your happiness. How attached are you to aspects of your situation? Does it frighten you to let go of these attachments? Try to make a vow to yourself right now to free yourself of one ego attachment. Think of the easiest thing to detach from. Perhaps you love designer handbags and use these to give you little moments of happiness. Think of an everlasting way, such as devotion to a meditation practice, you can use to replace this ego attachment, and make a promise to yourself today to do so.

If you desire true bliss, think of your plan to attain it. Perhaps you study more on meditative practices or methods of yoga. Perhaps you decide to read spiritual texts and works written by enlightened masters. What is your first step to become united with the part of you that exists only of unconditional love, joy, and peace?

Chapter 24: Monkey Mind

"Just as a monkey, swinging through a forest wilderness, grabs a branch. Letting go of it, it grabs another branch. Letting go of that, it grabs another one. Letting go of that, it grabs another one. In the same way, what's called 'mind,' 'intellect,' or 'consciousness' by day and by night arises as one thing and ceases as another."

Samyutta Nikaya 12.61"

A monkey mind is a term used to describe a mind that is restless, indecisive, whimsical, inconsistent, and erratic. Most people suffer from this monkey mind syndrome. It happens when we intend to do one thing and end up in a completely different direction. It happens when we lie awake at night worrying about the past or future. It happens in conversations when we stop listening to others and become engulfed in our own thoughts. It happens when we sit down to complete a project and end up on social media.

It has even been described by some as two drunken monkeys, chattering and fighting. Think of anytime you had to make a tough decision, were agitated, frustrated, or overwhelmed. During these states, did your thoughts sound something like a troop of noisy monkeys? This state of mind is the cause of unease. It is not the situations, but the way the mind tries to figure out and control situations that causes negative emotions. Learning to calm the monkey mind is the key to prevent the slough of negativity that invades our thoughts and disrupts our lives.

This sounds great in theory but is undoubtedly a challenge to put into practice. Just as you would train for a physical event, you must also train your mind to be ready when overwhelm strikes. Train during peaceful times with your mind is one, sober monkey instead of two wild, drunken ones. This will help you keep the monkeys calm when they are triggered. The two main ways to calm the monkey mind are through the practice of concentration and mediation.

Concentration can be practiced by focusing on one task at a time. When you are talking on the phone, concentrate only on that conversation and avoid the urge to check emails, pick up the house, or organize your desk. Practice working on one project for an extended period, perhaps set a timer for 60 minutes, and avoid engaging in any other activity for that entire time. We have conditioned our minds to try to focus on multiple tasks at once. The ability to multi-task has become a venerated skill and we feel uncomfortable only working on one thing at a time. This practice reinforces our unsettled minds and is counterproductive.

Meditation will also help calm the monkey mind, not only during the mediation but throughout the rest of your day. Developing a skill to calm the mind will carry over into all parts of your life, enabling you to develop greater concentration and avoid mental overwhelm. Meditation will also give insight into how many monkeys are chattering within your head. Try to sit in silence for 5-10 minutes and just observe the thoughts. You may begin to recognize reoccurring patterns that can be worked through after the mediation is complete and with enough practice you will eventually be able to sit for longer periods of time without the intrusion of your thoughts.

Meditation Activity: Try to sit for a period in silent mediation. Sit up, with your feet on the floor and your back straight and set a timer for 5-10 minutes. Focus on breathing in and out and try to quiet your mind. Observe what your mind does in this state. If you are not used to meditating in such a manner, your mind will become overactive, which is fine. It is not accustomed to sitting without stimulation and will rebel. When it does this, simply observe the thought and return your concentration back to the breath. With practice, your mind will quiet. This is also an activity you can easily implement anytime you feel overwhelmed. Set a timer for 5 minutes, close your eyes, silence your mind, and focus on your breath. You will find by taking this small amount of time to calm the monkey mind down, your mental state will become far clearer.

Concentration Activity: For today, be vigilant to only focus on one task at a time. If you are spending time with your family, avoid picking up your phone to check emails or social media. At work, set time aside to work on projects without checking email or taking breaks. During conversations, be fully present without allowing your mind to wander. This will cause some discomfort and urges will come up, but remind yourself why you cannot give into such urges. Your mental peace depends on it.

Chapter 25: Happiness

What does happiness mean to you? Take a moment to envision a happy life. What does this look like? Who is there? Where are you? What are you doing? How will you get there?

Now think of why these specific qualities lead to a happy life. What internal sensations would they produce? Perhaps a happy place for you is on a secluded island. It is not the island that causes the happy state but the feelings you associate with this serene environment. You may long for a deep sense of relaxation, peace, or a carefree life. When you think of who is there with you, often these people represent those who you love and whom love you the most. It is not the people, but the feeling of unconditional love that causes the feelings of happiness. If you visualize engaging in one of your favorite activities, it is not the activity that causes the happiness but the joy you feel.

When one breaks happiness down in such a manner it is easy to understand what qualities in life you think will bring you happiness. If you are searching for peace, you can find that anywhere, not just on a secluded island. Learn to be the love you wish to feel. Love yourself and others unconditionally, accept others as you would like to be accepted, and take time to express your love and gratitude for the people in your life. The people you love do not need to be around you for you to feel happy. Foster a permanent unconditional love in your heart and it will be with you always. If you want more joy, learn to look for the joy in all situations. You will find it in even the simplest of activities, if you learn to look for it.

When you can find happiness within, you will no longer yearn for outside factors to elicit happy emotions. We often foster a mindset that puts most of the control in outside situations and people. If someone treats you well, this will make you happy. If you can earn the success you want, this will make you happy. When you can travel more, this will make you happy. It is okay to have dreams, but in the journey to accomplishing your dreams, aim to find happiness in the process. This allows you to take back control. It will free you from fear. If something does not go as planned, you will be able to persevere while holding on to a happy state.

In many cultures, especially Western societies, this contradicts everything we have learned. Our culture promotes a false admiration for those who are rich, successful, and famous. We try to "keep up with the Joneses", a view that is strictly based on obtaining the outward appearance of happiness. The only way to achieve actual happiness is to forgo this ingrained thinking, learn what truly makes you happy, and focus your efforts on feeding your soul rather than your material desires.

Answer the questions listed in the beginning of this chapter, and write down the internal states that indicate a happy reality to you. Peace, love, bliss, freedom, etc. Once you have a list, try to foster these internal states in your daily activities. Consciously decide what you will do, how you will act, and what you will focus on today so you can achieve your desired internal happiness.

Part II
Powerful Meditation Techniques

Chapter 26: Introduction to Meditation

Meditation is an invaluable tool that leads to limitless possibilities. Our worlds are constantly filled with stimulation, our minds are rarely without thoughts, and feelings of anger, stress, anxiety, and depression are present on a daily basis. Meditation gives you a break from all of this. It helps you discover your path to happiness, purpose, and peace.

Its power is unlike any other tool for various reasons. First, it slows your mind down making it easier to observe your thinking patterns. This helps you understand what thoughts are causing particular emotions (fear, doubt) that prevent you from pursuing certain opportunities. It also helps with understanding what conditioned thinking patterns currently affect you in negative ways.

Second, meditation helps you communicate with your subconscious. Picture yourself in a crowded arena and you see a friend on the other side. You try to get his attention by shouting and waving your arms, yet because of all the noise and commotion your friend never sees you. Now, picture the arena is empty, and it is just you and him; he can easily see you and is able to hear everything you say. Your mind is the arena, and your subconscious is the friend on the other side. With all the constant chatter occurring in our minds, it can be impossible to communicate with the subconscious. Meditation removes the noise and makes this process much simpler.

Meditation also clears your mind so you can effectively ponder the source of true happiness, peace, and success. If you come home from a long day at work and have deadlines, finances, and an argument with a co-worker in your head, adding another task for your tired mind to process will be stress-inducing and seemingly impossible. You must clear out all of the junk before you can easily allow new thoughts to enter your consciousness.

Finally, meditation helps you directly connect with your higher self and the divine source. When we pray, we ask for help. When we meditate, we listen to the answer. Meditation empties your mind of negativity and egoism, allowing your intuition to guide you.

There are tons of different meditation techniques, with resources available everywhere. Developing a daily meditation will transform your life. It takes commitment but the results will be well worth the effort. Information on meditation can be found online, YouTube, or in books. You can also download mp3s or purchase CDs to get meditation music and directed or guided meditations. Below are brief descriptions of ten different techniques and instructions on how to implement them effectively.

Chapter 27:
10 Powerful Meditation Guides

Technique One: Mindful Meditation

Mindfulness meditation is the practice of clearing your mind and focusing on nothing but the here and now without judgment or trying to change anything. With the practice of daily meditation, it will be easier to control your stress and anxiety. You would not run a marathon without extensive training first, and mindfulness should be viewed similarly to any other training that helps you achieve the desired result. The more you work on it, the stronger your mindfulness power and endurance become. If you wish to develop a mindfulness meditation practice, it is best to start with shorter amounts of time and increase it. It is also best to pick the same time each day that you can commit to setting time aside to meditate. The more you can practice on a regular, consistent basis the better the overall results. Often people pick the morning to practice meditation or right before bed.

Mindful Meditation Steps:

1. Find a comfortable place to either lie straight or sit up. (Sometimes sitting can be better as you will not likely fall asleep).

2. Set a timer. When you start out, it is best to keep it around 10 minutes, but you can certainly increase this as you feel fit.

3. Begin to take calm breaths. Pay attention to how your breathing feels going in your nose, down your lungs and back out of your nose. Pay attention to how your chest or stomach rises and falls as your breath. The crucial component is not to try to change your breathing or make any judgments. This is not a deep breathing exercise. Breathe normally and merely focus your attention on your breath and body.

4. Next, do a body scan. Start with the top of your head. How does

it feel? What is the temperature? Can you feel your hair off your scalp? Now move down to your face. What do the back of your eyelids look like? How do your nose, lips, and chin feel? Continue this process down your entire body until you reach your toes. Pay attention to temperature and feeling. Notice if there is any tension or tightness but do not try to change or fix any sensation. You are simply noticing sensations and moving on.

5. After your body scan, pay attention to noises. First the sounds of your body. Can you hear your breathing? Focus just on that sound. Next, focus on the sounds in that room. What noises can you hear only in this space? Move on then to outside of that room, to the hallway or other areas of your living space. What noises can you hear? Finally, focus your attention past your living space to the outside. Can you hear anything?

6. Finally, pay attention to how it feels to be at that very moment. Let any thought that comes into your mind float out. Do not judge yourself for falling out of a mindfulness state and do not judge any thought that comes into your head. Do not attach any emotion to anything. Simply focus on sensations. A thought is solely a thought that floats in and out when no attention is paid to it.

7. If you find that one technique works best for you then carry out the rest of the meditation using that technique, if not just "be" until your timer rings.

Technique Two: Breathing Meditation

This is a great meditation for beginners. It helps to both focus and calm the mind, as well as physically relax the body. There are many different ways that you can engage in this type of meditation. It is best to set a timer so that you can focus exclusively on breathing without worrying about the time. It is a beneficial technique to engage in anytime you feel overwhelmed and is exceptionally easy because it can be done anywhere.

To prepare for the meditation, you can lie down or sit in a chair with your eyes open or closed. For a deeper relaxation, sitting or lying in a quiet space with your eyes closed is recommended. Take deep inhales into your diaphragm (your stomach) and exhale fully until all air is emptied from your body. Make sure that the breath is rhythmic and consistent each cycle (i.e. you breathe in and out for the same length of time each round). We are used to taking shallow breaths, into our chest, especially when we are under stress. Under stress our breathing can also be inconsistent, perhaps you take four shallow breaths, followed by one deep breath, followed by five shallow breaths, so on. During this meditation, inhale deeply until your belly rises and exhale fully as your stomach collapses and pulls in; the length of each breath is not nearly as important as the consistency throughout the meditation. Below is a brief list of different types of breathing you can engage in, but there are countless others that you can easily research:

1. Inhale/Hold/Exhale at Same Count: Inhale 4 count, hold 4 count, exhale 4 count, hold 4 count, repeat

2. Exhale Longer than Inhale: Inhale 5 count, Hold 6 count, Exhale 7 count, Hold 6 count, repeat

3. Visualized Breathing: Picture a cleansing blue color clearing your mind and body as you inhale and picture a red color as you exhale all of your built up stress, anxiety, doubt and any other negative feelings.

Technique Three: Progressive Muscle Relaxation

This is a meditation technique designed to fully relax your body. Your mind will also be focused on your body and not easily able to wander. There are 2 steps in this mediation, the first is to tense and contract your muscles and the second is to relax those same muscles. It is best to find a comfortable place and lie down in order to fully relax.

During this meditation, you will be working with all the major muscle groups in your body. To make it easy to remember, start with your feet and systematically move up or if you prefer, you can do it in the reverse order, from your forehead down to your feet. You can also choose to focus on each side of the body separately (for example tense left foot, relax, then tense the right foot, and relax) or together (tense both feet at the same time, then relax both at the same time). Use the below steps as a guide to first tighten each muscle, hold the contraction for a count of 1-5 seconds, and release fully:

1. Feet (curl your toes downward, point your toes), Hold, and Relax

2. Lower leg and foot (tighten your calf muscle by pulling toes towards you), Hold, and Relax

3. Entire leg (squeeze thigh muscles while doing above), Hold, and Relax

4. Hands (clench your fists), Hold, and Relax

5. Arms (tighten your biceps and forearms while clenching fist), Hold, and Relax

6. Buttocks (clench your buttocks together), Hold, and Relax

7. Stomach (pull your stomach in), Hold, and Relax

8. Chest (tighten entire chest), Hold, and Relax

9. Neck and shoulders (shrug your shoulders up to your ears), Hold, and Relax

10. Mouth (open your mouth wide), Hold, and Relax

11. Eyes (clench your eyelids tightly), Hold, and Relax

12. Forehead (raise your eyebrows), Hold, and Relax

13. Finish with Entire Body Tension, Hold, and Relax

Note: If you have any injuries, heart problems or other medical issues, consult your doctor before engaging in this activity.

Technique Four: Guided Meditation and Visualization

Guided meditations are another great tool for beginners. During this, you listen to an audio guiding you deep into meditation. There are plenty available for free on YouTube or recordings available to purchase. You can also guide yourself through a meditation using your own thoughts, although it may be harder to relax and let go than if you were to listen to pre-recorded one. There are guided meditations specifically for commutating with your subconscious and for releasing old, negative thinking patterns. These are very similar to hypnosis, and some guided meditations will be labeled as hypnosis when searching online. The key to receiving the most benefit is to allow yourself to be open to deep relaxation and the suggestions stated in these guided meditations. The deeper you go in the meditation, the more positive effects you will experience.

Sample Guided Visualization

(Read through this guide and then sit or lie with your eyes closed and mentally go through these images. Use your imagination and fully immerse yourself in the visualization. Set a timer or use this to help drift off to sleep.)

Imagine you are walking in a field. The grass is soft, the sun is warm, and a soft breeze blows gently against your skin. Take in all the sights, listen to any noises, and feel the sun and wind against your body as you walk.

In a distance, you see a staircase and begin to walk towards it. As you approach the staircase, you notice that ten stairs descend into a dark, cool abyss. You know relaxation awaits at the bottom of the stairs. Take your first step down and feel a sense of warmth, peace, and relaxation overcome you. Count each of the ten steps as you descend, and with each passing step feel a deeper sense of relaxation.

As you reach the bottom of the staircase, you feel sand beneath your feet. You are in a dark, cool tunnel and see a light in the distance. Walk towards the light. As you do, you begin to hear sounds of crashing waves, sea gulls and smell salt in the air. Finally, you reach the end of the tunnel and see the beautiful sea. It radiates magnificent colors as the mighty sun glistens upon it. Walk to the edge of the shore and sit down. The sand is soft and warm. The sun kisses your skin and the ocean air breezes through your hair. As you look around, you notice there are no other people or buildings as far as you can see. The only sights are of birds, dolphins, fish and the beautiful colors radiating from the vast ocean.

Take in these sights, the sounds, and the smells and know you are safe here. A black box floats up to you and you know this is a place where you can put all of your worries. Pour every worry you are holding into this black box. Shut the box and send it out into the ocean. Watch the worry-filled box float far out until you can no longer see it and know in this moment you are safe, fully relaxed and free of all worries, fears and negativity. Bask in this feeling. Stay here as long as you want.

After sitting on the beach for some time, you know it is time to return to the world. Get up and head back to the tunnel. Walk through the tunnel until you reach the staircase. Slowly ascend each step and feel more energized and positive as you do. Count each step from one to ten and once you reach the tenth step you are ready to tackle your day. Keep this beautiful beach in your heart throughout the rest of your day and know you can come back to it any time you desire.

Technique Five: Mantras

Mantras are simply words or phrases used to aid in concentration during meditation. Using mantras will help focus your mind, enabling you to sit in stillness without the intrusion of distracting thoughts. Mantras are also said to help alter the subconscious, raise your energy, and expand awareness to reach spiritual states of consciousness.

The mantra you choose depends on the goal of your meditation. You can choose a word or phrase that is meaningful to you, such as "happy", "let is go", or "I am at peace". You can also look to spiritual texts for mantras that are said to elicit higher states of consciousness. Two popular mantras used in yoga, are the words "om", which is said to be the sound of creation, and "shanti", which simply means peace. Many put them together in the mantra "Om shanti, shanti, shanti." This mantra can help with manifesting, raising energy, expressing gratitude, and welcoming peace.

When using a mantra in meditation, sit or lie in stillness and focus solely on the mantra. Some mantras are intended to be spoken, as the vibrations are said to elicit a spiritual state. Others can be said silently. You can repeat mantras as you breathe or you can incorporate the mantra into your breath. For example, you may say "I am" with each inhale and "happy" during each exhale. There are no strict rules and regulations for mantras; simply find one that works for you and concentrate on it during the course of each meditation.

<u>*List of Mantras:*</u>

Sanskrit Mantras (used in India, Hinduism, Yoga)

Om: Say aloud and feel the vibration radiate from your root chakra (located at the base of the spine) up and through your spiritual eye (the point between the eyebrows).

Shanti: Say or sing it to affirm peace within oneself and to send peace to others.

Ah: Take a deep breath in and as you exhale, open your mouth wide while you say "Ahhhhh". Keep the focus of your eyes at the spiritual eye and feel the vibrations travel up the chakras. This has been said to help with manifesting and should be done in the morning.

Buddhist Mantras

Derived from The Buddha Center

Om Mani Padme Hum: Say out loud or silently for blessings and compassion.

Om Amideva Hrīh [OM AMI DEWA HRIH]: Say to overcome all obstacles & hindrances, find protection from dangers, and overcome blocks to success.

Om Tare Tuttare Ture Soha: Use to overcome physical, mental, emotional and relationship blockages.

Modern Meditation Mantras

I am love.

I am calm.

I am at peace.

I am joy.

I am in the flow.

I am one with the divine.

I surround myself with love, peace, and joy.

I am loved.

I am enough.

I am connected.

Technique Six: Energy and Manifesting

Manifesting or 'Law of Attraction' meditation is rooted in the belief that everything is energy, and by aligning with this energy, we can attract what we desire. Before beginning such a meditation, you must fully embrace this idea. It is essential to have faith in energetic laws and a belief in your ability to attract energy to you. Doubt will only interfere with the energetic flow and may even cause you to attract unwanted circumstances.

To begin your manifesting mediation, sit or lie and start to silence your mind. It often helps to begin with a few minutes of mantras or breathing exercises until you are in a relaxed and centered state.

Once in a relaxed state, feel your connection to your higher self and to the universe. Visualize your energy expanding past your physical body, through your higher self and connecting with the divine source.

After you feel a connection with divinity, focus on what you want to attract into your life. Imagine it in detail. Picture yourself already having your desire. Visualize your energy spanning out and attracting exactly what you want. Imagine how this desire will not only help you, but will also benefit others.

Now envision the feelings your desire will produce. Desires are often covers for unmet emotional needs. Money often indicates a desire for security. Material goods often indicate a desire for happiness. Success often indicates a desire for freedom. Feel your desired emotions take over your entire being. And finally trust the universe will provide you with your desires, in a manner that supports your highest and best good.

Technique Seven: Raise Your Consciousness

The original purpose of meditation was to expand one's awareness and develop a better connection with the divine. Modern meditations have evolved to meet a variety of needs, but the deepest, most spiritual meditations continue to be rooted in this ideal.

To raise consciousness, one must expand past the limited confines of the human body and recognize s/he is one with the infinite, just a tiny part of a greater reality, and shares a connection with all other beings. Imagine yourself as one bulb on an infinite string of lights. You do not shine any brighter nor are you more or less important than any other bulb. You are also not the source of your light and without a divine plug and outlet, you will not shine at all. Everyone in the universe represents one bulb and the source is the same for us all.

Expansion of consciousness can be accomplished in a variety of ways. The simplest way is to meditate, with your focus on the spiritual eye, and envision a connection with the divine source. Feel the connection pulling you out of your limited reality and connecting you with everything else in the universe. Visualize a white light pouring into you, through your crown chakra (the top of your head). Now envision this light flowing through your entire being and radiating out. It flows down your body, through the bottom of your feet, and connects you to mother earth. You are simultaneously grounded to the center of the earth and expanded past all imaginable elements of the universe.

Feel a sense of unconditional love and bliss as the divine encompasses your being. Bask in this sensation during your meditation and carry the feeling with you everywhere, recognizing the same divinity is in everyone.

Technique Eight: Love, Joy, and Peace Meditation

Love, joy, and peace are three of the highest energy vibrations, according to Dr. Hawkin's *Scale of Consciousness*. We are all energetic beings, constantly vibrating at frequencies that match our thoughts, actions, and intentions. Your energetic vibration is determined by your emotion, and since our emotions vary throughout the day, so do the frequencies we emit. In this meditation, you will raise your vibration as well as share this high vibration with the world.

Begin by relaxing your mind with a few mantras or deep breaths. In a relaxed state, begin to imagine people and pets you love. Feel the unconditional love you have for them. Feel this love expand from your heart and fill your entire body.

Next, imagine people, places or events that bring you pure joy. Also, imagine others close to you being in a state of pure joy. Allow this joy to overwhelm you. Think of your dreams coming true. Imagine others' dreams coming true. Feel unwavering happiness fill your soul at these thoughts.

Finally, visualize the most peaceful situation you can imagine. Perhaps you are at the beach, a lake, or simply in your favorite part of the house. Feel the peace of this situation take over your entire body. Imagine those close to you also developing the same feelings of peace and tranquility. Sit for a while and enjoy this worry-free, calm state.

Once your body is filled with love, joy, and peace allow these vibrations to expand to the room you are in, enveloping anyone or anything in this room. Next, expand them to incase your entire house or building, then your community and city, then your state and country, and finally envision these high vibrations encompassing the entire world with love, joy, and peace.

After you have completed the meditation, set an intention to continue to focus on love, peace, and joy the rest of your day and share these vibrations with everyone you encounter.

Technique Nine: Anchoring

Anchoring is a Neuro-Linguistic Programming, NLP, technique used to induce a frame of mind or emotion. It is a conditioning that develops when a person evokes an emotion and pairs it with a gesture or touch of some kind. To do this get into a meditative state. Use breathing, mindfulness or any combination to begin. Then think of an emotion you want to condition. This could be success, happiness, fulfillment or relaxation. Now picture a time in your life when you experienced the desired emotion. If you aspire to feel successful, think of a time in your life when you experienced success. Perhaps, it was when your football team won the state championship in high school, or you got the top grade in the class during college. Picture the moment vividly and experience the emotions as if they are currently happening. While feeling the emotion, hold your thumb and index finger together. Relax for a few seconds then reimagine this experience with a heightened state of emotion and again bring your thumb and index finger together. Repeat this process 3-5 additional times. If you repeat this exercise daily, eventually when you put your thumb and index finger together you will experience the emotion, no matter the circumstance.

You can use this technique to recondition your thinking. For example, if you anchor a feeling of success, anytime you experience doubt or feelings of overwhelm, you can use your anchor to stimulate a positive, successful state. Anchoring can be used in conjunction with other visualization techniques as well. For example, once your anchor is set you can visualize yourself being successful in your current or future pursuits. Engage the anchor by placing your thumb and finger together and experience the emotional response of success, making your visualization more real.

Technique Ten: Imprinting New Beliefs

In this technique, you will get into a meditative state, with any of the exercises listed above and say a set of affirmations. Use the same set of statements every time and try to feel as if these affirmations are true. Somedays you may believe them and others your ego and lower-self may step in and call you a liar. It doesn't matter. The important part is that you are imprinting new beliefs into your subconscious. Do this for at least 5 minutes every day for a minimum of 30 days to start to see some results.

<u>*Affirmation Examples*</u>

I am amazing.

I am loved.

I am respected.

I am accomplished.

I am successful.

I am abundant.

I am happy.

I am confident.

I am brave.

I am at peace.

I am balanced.

I am inspired.

I am deserving of all my dreams.

Others look up to me.

I love myself.

I am always enough.

I am filled with confidence, self-esteem and love.

I easily accept that which I cannot change.

I fully accept every part of myself.

I am wonderfully unique.

I fully accept myself now and am always growing in all aspects of my life.

I radiate positivity and love.

I am free of all guilt, shame, resentment and anger.

My unique characteristics lead me to my perfect life.

Conclusion

The daily practice of reflection and meditation leads to a more intentional approach to life. You become the director of your own feature film, instead of an extra in everyone else's. Carry these reflection practices with you as you continue on your journey. Each day you live in an intentional, reflective manner is a step closer to a life of peace, fulfillment and genuine happiness. You are worth the time and effort it takes to transform your life. Be kind to yourself through the process. Be understanding of resistance and setbacks, and remain confident you can meet and overcome any challenge. Continue to see the beauty in life, in others, and in yourself. You have made a commitment to evolve past the narrow constructs of society. Those who embark on such a path feel drawn to a life that offers more than the one they fell into. Such a path is not understood by many and those who pursue it accomplish a life lived by only a few. So go against the grain, create your path, and make sure to embrace each moment along the way.

30 Day Mindfulness Challenge

*Step-By-Step Guide
to
Living a Stress-Free
&
Happy Life*

by

Rachael L. Thompson

Challenge Introduction

Welcome to the 30 Day Mindfulness Challenge! This is a time to push yourself, become open to change, and see the transformation unfold. Every day there will be a new challenge, a description of the challenge, and some tips and action steps. It is a good idea to read the challenge for the following day the evening before to prepare and again the morning of as a refresher. The daily activities each week will build on one another and will gradually become more challenging. It is important not to skip a day so you do not miss any necessary skills needed for future activities.

The challenge is broken into four, weekly sections, with one bonus day to begin the challenge and another to end the challenge. Each week has a different focus to facilitate optimal learning at each stage of mindful skill development.

In week one, we will focus solely on building a meditation practice. Meditation allows you to practice mindfulness when it is easy. It also gives insight into the chaos that occurs within your own head. We all have tons of thoughts popping up every minute that cause fluctuations in mood, feelings, and behaviors. Meditation simply shines a light on how your brain works. Once you have this understanding and some basic tools to slow your monkey mind down, you will then be able to apply mindfulness to everyday tasks.

During the second week of the challenge, you will get a chance to apply mindfulness to simple tasks. You need to train for mindfulness, so envision this week as running one mile at a time when you are training for a 5k race. With each day, that mile becomes easier to run and by week three you are able to add a little distance.

Week three will focus on broad mindfulness concepts. You will be encouraged to apply mindfulness to increase awareness, compassion, love, and appreciation. All of the concepts are explained and you will be given concrete action steps to apply them into your life.

Finally, we will dedicate week four to expanding and practicing everything you learned. This week will focus on increasing the amount and duration of learned mindfulness techniques. In this week, you will get to apply everything you have been practicing and reflect on how far you have come in less than a month.

By using this challenge as a guide, you will begin to transform your life in a short period of time. You may notice a decrease in anger, anxiety, or frustration while increasing your awareness and appreciation for all of life's moments. You will be able to develop a new perspective of life that leads to greater amounts of happiness and peace.

If you would like background information on mindfulness, check out **Beginners Guide to Mindfulness in a World of Chaos**. This books breaks down the concept of mindfulness in today's world and gives you essential guidelines to apply it effectively into your life.

CONTENTS

30 DAY Mindfulness Challenge Week One

Week one will focus solely on meditation. Developing a meditation practice will help you develop mindfulness skills you can then apply in everyday situations. After week 1, there will not be any specific meditations laid out in the challenge but you are encouraged to continue incorporating a daily meditation practice into your weeks.

The daily meditations will focus on being mindful for a period of time yet each one will be slightly different. You may find some are easier, others are challenging, and some feel more comfortable for you. Going forward, you will have all the different types of meditation in your toolbox and can choose which ones you want to use. You decide each day how long you will meditate. Remember to start small. Once you feel you can be mindful for the entire duration of the meditation, increase the amount of time by a few minutes each practice. Remember that certain days will be better than others. The key is to not judge yourself; it is all part of the growing process. Let's get started!

Bonus Day: The Pre-Test Mindful Day

During this first week, you will have 8 days, as this first day is a bonus day! This will be a pre-test to gauge how mindful you are before starting this journey. You will repeat this during the first days of weeks 2 and 3 and after the completion of the challenge.

For the entire day, just be mindful of how you navigate the world. Pay attention to what you think, feel, and how you act and respond to situations. The goal is to be aware without any judgment or trying to change anything.

Example: When driving, be mindful of what you think about. Do you feel the urge to listen to a certain type of music or podcast? When you get to work, be mindful of the conversations you engage in and what thoughts and feelings occur as a result. Again, this is not the time to try to change anything but just take note of your own behaviors.

This Mindful Day will be like falling in and out of a dream. You will be mindful for a while and then will slip back into a non-mindful state. Once you realize you slipped back into this "dream" state, simply bring your attention back to the present. Do not get discouraged or try to change your behavior in any way, just observe.

DAY 1: Mindful Body Meditation

Preparation: *Sit or lie in a comfortable position. Set a timer for 5-10 minutes. Take 5 slow, deep, calming breaths to get you into your meditative state.*

Mindful Awareness

In this meditation you will be doing a body scan, focusing on the sensations of each part of your body.

Focus on: Temperature, external sensations of clothing, air, feeling hair, the pressure of body weight, and internal sensations of tightness and relaxation.

Spend anywhere from 10-30 seconds focusing on each, individual area. Once you have noted all of the sensations, move to the next body part. Start your focus on the bottom of the feet. Move up to the ankles, calves/shins, front and back of knees, front and back of thighs, hips, bottom and pelvic area, lower back and lower stomach, middle back and middle stomach, top back and chest, shoulders, neck, back of head, face, and top of the head.

Note: For this meditation, you can choose to end it once you have scanned your entire body instead of setting a timer.

DAY 2: Mindful Breathing Meditation

Preparation: *Sit or lie in a comfortable position. Set a timer for 5-10 minutes. Take 5 slow, deep, calming breaths to get you into your meditative state.*

Breathing Awareness

After your 5 initial calming breaths, begin to breathe normally. Focus on the feeling of the air coming into your nose (or mouth). Notice the temperature (typically it is cool). Feel the air as it travels down your airway into your lungs. Feel your chest and/or stomach rise as your lungs fill up. Notice the fall of your chest and stomach as you begin to exhale. Feel the air coming back up your passageway. Feel the sensations and temperatures as you exhale through your nose or mouth. Can you feel the air on your face? What is the temperature?

Continue this process for the remainder of the mediation. Do not try to change your breathing pattern. Simply pay attention to the sensations of the breathing. If you notice your thoughts start to wander, simply bring your attention back to your breathing.

DAY 3: Mindful Sound Meditation

Preparation: *Sit or lie in a comfortable position. Set a timer for 5-10 minutes. Take 5 slow, deep, calming breaths to get you into your meditative state.*

Sound Awareness

During this meditation, you will only focus your attention on the sounds you hear. Pay attention without attaching any judgment (positive or negative) to them. For example, if you hear a loud dump truck outside do not label it as loud or annoying. If you, on the other hand, hear the sound of a bird chirping, do not label this as pretty or relaxing. The point is not to pay attention to "peaceful" sounds but to pay attention to all noises without labeling them.

Start with the sounds of your breath and body. Focus only on these subtle sounds for a few moments without trying to change anything.

Next focus only on sounds you hear in the room you are sitting or lying down in. No room is completely silent. You may hear noises from your air conditioning or heat, from different appliances, or noises from any other people or pets in the house. It may be helpful to focus on one noise at a time. Focus on the noise of appliances first, then pay attention to the sound of your dog breathing, then pay attention to the sound of your kids playing, so on.

Finally, focus your attention on all the noises you hear coming from the outside. These can be animals, cars, people, or the wind. Again, it can be helpful to focus on one noise at a time. Hold your focus on each noise for a few second before scanning for another noise to listen to.

DAY 4: Mindful Hand Meditation

Preparation: *Sit or lie in a comfortable position. Set a timer for 5-10 minutes. Take 5 slow, deep, calming breaths to get you into your meditative state.*

Hand Focus

This will be the first meditation that focuses on "being" without concentrating on different stimuli. During this, you will only focus on your hands.

Begin by paying attention to the positioning of your hands and each one of your fingers. Note the temperature of each individual finger. Focus on the weight of your hands against the surface they are lying on. If there is anything covering them or touching them, notice that sensation.

Now allow yourself to just be still. When you notice your thoughts start to drift, always bring your attention back to your hands. You do not have to focus on them the entire time, but they will help you be mindful as your mind tries to take over the mediation.

DAY 5: Mindful Head Meditation

Preparation: *Sit or lie in a comfortable position. Set a timer for 5-10 minutes. Take 5 slow, deep, calming breaths to get you into your meditative state.*

Head Focus

For this meditation, you will focus on the sensations of your head. Typically we associate the head with a place where thoughts are constantly being fired off, but in this meditation, you will focus only on the sensations and feel what it is like to have a peaceful head space.

Feel the sensation of the top of your head. Temperature, hair follicles, etc. Move down to your forehead and repeat. Next feel your eyelids closed over your eyes. What do you see? Move down to your nose and feel your breath moving in and out. Move down to your lips. Notice if they are closed or open and if they are tense or relaxed. Finally, pay attention to any sensations of your chin. Move now to the back of your head. What sensations do you feel? Is there pressure or weight? Finally, pay attention to the inside of your head without any thoughts. Are there any sensations? Keep this mindful focus until the end of the meditation.

DAY 6: Mindful Sensation Meditation

Preparation: *Sit or lie in a comfortable position. Set a timer for 5-10 minutes. Take 5 slow, deep, calming breaths to get you into your meditative state.*

Body Sensations

Focus on the sensations of your body as a whole. Feel its weight. Feel its temperature. Feel any sensations inside of it. Feel any sensations outside of it. Do not judge any sensation. Focus on your body being present in the moment.

When your mind starts to wander, bring your attention back to the sensations. If it helps, you can pick one part (i.e. legs) or one sensation (i.e. the feeling of clothing against skin) to bring your attention back when your thoughts start to wonder.

DAY 7: Just Be Meditation

Preparation: *Sit or lie in a comfortable position. Set a timer for 5-10 minutes. Take 5 slow, deep, calming breaths to get you into your meditative state.*

Mindful Being

During this mediation, do not focus your attention on anything at all. Practice sitting or lying still. When any sensations arise, try not to judge them or move.

Example, if you feel the urge to shift your body because a thought arises that said you were getting uncomfortable, let this thought pass through your head without acting on it.

When any thoughts arise let them pass through as clouds. If you get caught in a thought story, let it pass as soon as you notice, and remain still. Thoughts are nothing more than thoughts. They do not define you. They are not the truth and you do not need to act on them. You are a being who is separate from your thoughts. Sit in this state of being through the entire meditation.

30 DAY Mindfulness Challenge Week 2

This week will focus on adding mindfulness to your daily tasks. There will be no meditation, but you are encouraged to incorporate 5-10 minutes of mindful meditation in addition to this week's activities.

Week two will be slightly more challenging than the previous week and the activities are meant as building blocks for living a more mindful life. Each day focuses on a new mindful activity. Do not feel pressure to practice the exercises from the previous day(s) during the current day, instead focus on being as mindful as possible during each new daily activity.

DAY 1: Mindful Day

This is a repeat of the first day of the challenge. It is always important to periodically gauge where you are in your mindfulness journey. Pay special attention to times when you feel negative emotions or have a hard time being mindful.

For the entire day, just be mindful of how you navigate the world. Pay attention to what you think, feel, and how you act and respond to situations. The goal is to be aware without any judgment or trying to change anything.

Example: When driving, be mindful of what you think about. Do you feel the urge to listen to a certain type of music or podcast? When you get to work, be mindful of the conversations you engage in and what thoughts and feelings occur as a result.

Again, this is not the time to try to change anything but just take note of your own behaviors. This Mindful Day will be like falling in and out of a dream. You will be mindful for a while and then will slip back into a non-mindful state. Once you realize you slipped back into this "dream" state, simply bring your attention back to the present. Do not get discouraged or try to change your behavior in any way.

DAY 2: Mindful Relaxing

Today, set aside some time to mindfully relax. Instead of sitting down and looking at your phone, browsing the internet, or turning on the TV, dedicate at least the first 10 minutes to sitting still. Apply what you learned during your meditations but this time in an aware, non-meditative state.

This is your time to enjoy your relaxation instead of trying to distract your mind. Feel the sensations in your body. Is anything tense or sore? Does any part feel especially relaxed? Listen to the sounds and observe the sights. Any thoughts that come to your mind, let them peacefully float out. Remind yourself that this time is for relaxing and anything that you need to think about or handle can be done at a later time. Practice this every time you plan to "take a break" and relax today.

If you have an opportunity to go outside, enjoy all the sights and sounds of nature. If you have time to watch your children play, savor every moment without allowing yourself to become preoccupied with something else. You will find that this type of relaxation calms your mind rather than distracting it.

DAY 3: Mindful Conversations

Anytime you have a conversation with someone today, be mindful throughout the entire experience. Listen to everything being said without thinking how you are going to respond. Also, be mindful when you are talking. If anything said elicits a feeling, note it and be mindful of what thoughts prompted that feeling. Do not, however, allow this to take away from you being mindful during the conversation. Just note the experience and you can reflect on it after the conversation has finished.

For example, if talking to a co-worker about your boss provokes feelings of anger, make a note of it and do your best to bring your awareness back to the present conversation instead of focusing on your thoughts. After the conversation, think about what exactly was said and the thoughts that came up that caused the anger. (Note: Tomorrow there will be more discussion and time to practice this technique).

If others are having a conversation but you are not an active participant at the moment, listen without placing any judgments or thoughts on what you hear. Allow the words others are saying to enter and exit your awareness without holding on to any piece you heard.

DAY 4: Mindfully Combat Negativity

Today you are going to be the observer of your emotions as if you are a doctor studying a patient. It may be beneficial to keep a thought journal to track your emotions and thoughts.

Pay attention to any time you have a negative emotion, such as anger, resentment, sadness, frustration, annoyance, anxiety, depressive feelings, guilt, etc. As soon as you notice the emotion, be mindful of what you are thinking. Outside factors never cause negative feelings. It is the thought attached to the situation that causes the feelings. Understanding what thoughts you are attaching to situations will help you understand where your negativity comes from and also help reduce it. Often we have a negative feeling and then attach more thoughts to support the negative feeling which in turn increases its intensity. By simply taking a step back, and being mindful of your thoughts and the situation, you are able to stop this process before it gets out of control.

When you have trouble getting out of a negative mindset, focus on being mindful in the current situation. Use techniques from meditation to help with this. Think of it as riding your bike down a steep hill. The top of the hill is the environment, then a negative thought comes along and gives you a little push down the hill. This hill can be very small or it can be gigantic. If you allow your mind and emotions to take over, you continue to pick up momentum and before you realize, you are speeding down a hill, out of control, with no way of stopping yourself. Now, if you insert mindfulness immediately after that push, the ground begins to level and you realize it was just a small hill and you quickly regain control.

Today, focus on being mindful as soon as you feel any negativity. Take the situation for what it is, pay attention to your thoughts, and you will notice this can quickly begin to lessen your negative emotions. Bring your focus to the present moment (sights, sounds, etc.). This will help stop you from rolling down that hill of negativity

DAY 5: Mindful Walking

If you are able, schedule a mindful walk for yourself today. Make sure the walk is at least 10-15 minutes and try to be mindful the entire time. If you are unable to schedule this walk, make sure anytime you walk today you are mindful. This can be a walk from your car to a building, a walk from the couch to the refrigerator, or a walk to the next cubical at your office. It does not matter how long or short, just make it mindful.

Check in with your body: How does it feel when you are walking? What can you hear and see during this time? What does it feel like for your feet every time you take a step? As always, do not allow any thoughts that creep in to stay. Do not judge, good or bad, anything you experience. If your feet hurt from a long day, focus on just the sensation and do not label it as pain. If you take your dog for a walk and he begins to pull, do not label him as a bad dog for doing so. If you see someone wearing a nice watch, do not think you like the watch. Objectively observe. It is just a sensation in your feet, your dog is pulling and you feel sensations in your hand as you restrain him, and it is not a nice watch, it is just a watch.

If you find you fall back into old habits and place judgments on anything, never dwell on it. Dwelling only comes from placing judgments on yourself. It comes from thinking about past events, so always remind yourself to stay in the present. That moment has already passed and every moment is a time to refocus on your mindfulness.

DAY 6: Mindful Commute

Anytime you travel or commute today, plan to be mindful. This could be your commute to and from work, it can be driving the kids to school, it can be running errands or going to the gym. It also does not have to be when you are driving. If you bike or walk to places, be mindful during those activities. If you take public transportation, also remember to be mindful.

During any of these commutes, practice all of the sensation-focusing exercises you used during your meditation practices. Do not listen to any music, news, or podcasts. Just let your mind become aware of all the sensations you are feeling, hearing, seeing, and smelling.

If commute with other people, be mindful of all conversations during this time. Listen to everything being said without thinking how you are going to respond to it. If others are having a conversation, listen but without placing any judgments or thoughts on what you are hearing. Allow the words others are saying to enter and exit your awareness without holding on to anything.

If you struggle with anger while driving or comminuting, this is the perfect time to implement the mindful techniques discussed during Day 4 (Mindfully Combatting Negativity). Read through those instructions again to help remind you of the techniques.

DAY 7: Mindful Meals

Be mindful anytime you eat today. Do not engage in activities that distract your mind, such as watching TV, texting, or surfing the internet. If you are around others and engaging in conversation, make sure you remain mindful of the eating process.

With every bite of food, taste the flavors, feel the textures and temperatures, and hear the sounds. Feel the food traveling to your stomach as you swallow it. Do the same any time you take a drink. Pay attention to how your body feels as you eat or any thoughts that may pop into your head.

When do you notice you are getting full and have had enough nourishment to stop eating? You will likely find it takes you longer to eat this way and some people eat less as they notice they get full much earlier than usual.

30 DAY Mindfulness Challenge Week Three

During week three, we will look at mindfulness in a less concrete, more esoteric manner. By now, you have built some mindfulness muscles through meditation and activities and are ready to apply these skills to broader concepts. This week we will focus on emotions, perspective, and habits.

It is time to explore how you interact with your world. Act as an unbiased observer of your own thoughts, feelings, and behaviors. There will be time to work on anything you find hinders your life or goals, but one must first truly understand patterns before any effective changes can be made. Over the next seven day, you will get a chance to explore and discover your natural patterns.

Note: There will be no meditation, but you are encouraged to incorporate 5-15 minutes of mindful meditation in addition to this week's activities.

DAY 1: Mindful Compassion

Have you ever paid attention to how you perceive others? It can be our natural inclination to view others as they relate to us. We hear a horrific story on the news about a family being murdered and feel compassion as we think about it happening to our own family.

A lack of compassion is also a result of our self-involved tendencies. You lack compassion for your best friend who is going through a divorce because it means that you will get to see her more often. These true feelings are something we try to mask from others and even from ourselves as nobody likes to admit any potential character flaw.

Today, pay attention to your true feelings towards other people. After you become aware of these feelings, be mindful of the root of each feeling. Do not judge yourself, and more importantly, do not try to deny or cover-up your natural feelings. Be honest and simply observe. This will give insight into your true compassion for others and what self-serving needs you may be trying to meet with this compassion or lack of compassion.

DAY 2: Mindful Happiness

When was the last time you thought about what truly makes you happy in life? In addition, have you ever asked yourself why these are sources of your happiness? Finally, how often do you experience happiness?

Through mindfulness, you are able to explore what exactly makes you happy and ideally learn how you can increase overall happiness. It may also be quite eye opening how much of your day is spent in a state of unhappiness.

There are three activities today. The first is to observe how often you feel happy and what you are doing when you experience this happiness.

Second, pay attention to what activities cause unhappiness and be mindful of your thoughts surrounding those situations.

Third, take some time to ponder what makes you happy and ask yourself "why?" Mindfully explore what needs are being met and what exactly causes the happiness. For example, if gardening leads to happiness, perhaps it is because your mind is focused on that one task or you enjoy being out in nature. The more you are aware of what exactly increases happiness, the more you can add in similar activities.

It may be helpful to write down everything you observe about your happiness today. By doing so, you will easily be able to spot patterns you were unaware of prior to today.

DAY 3: Mindful Love

Love is an emotion associated with the heart, not the head. The term mindful love may seem like a bit of an oxymoron, but the mind plays a much larger role in the feeling of love than may be apparent.

Think now of who you love. (Partners, children, family, friends, pets). Why do you love them?

Think of what you love. (The beach, chocolate, bonfires, wine). Why do you love these things?

The mind can also distract us from fully experiencing love. How many times have you been with your loved ones and been distracted by your thoughts?

For today, embrace each loving moment you spend. Try to engage in an activity you love or be around someone you love. This can be as simple as eating a piece of chocolate while sitting next to your loving cat. During this time, be fully present in your thoughts and feelings towards the object of your love.

Make sure to eliminate all expectations prior. Do not expect your children to behave because you decided to embrace their presence. Rather, sit in a mindful state and pay attention to how different the experience is than usual. You may even find you become more tolerant and far less reactive as you focus on loving thoughts instead of negativity or frustration.

DAY 4: Mindful Judgement

Everyone judges, yet these judgments are rarely a true reflection of reality. We often have tendencies and subconscious biases that drastically affect our ability to accurately view our environment.

Today, focus on every judgment you make. These can be judgments about yourself, other people, and situations. You likely will discover patterns. Many tend to judge others harshly; they naturally jump to negative conclusions. Some want to give everyone the benefit of the doubt. Others judge themselves harshly in comparison to everyone else.

Our judgments affect our moods, actions, and well-being. Someone who automatically judges all situations as potentially dangerous likely suffers from high levels of anxiety. A person who suffers from perfectionism likely has underlying insecurities and self-doubt.

Remember not to judge your judgments, but just observe. Observe how judgments affect your feelings and decisions. Also, be mindful of any patterns or a natural outlook you hold that affects how you automatically judge situations.

DAY 5: Mindful Intent

Today's focus will be on your intentions. We all act with an intended purpose, yet we are often unaware what our true intentions are. For example, if you yell at your spouse for neglecting to take out the trash, the intention for yelling may not be as clear as you first think. With some mindful observation, you may find your true intent was to hurt him in an attempt to make yourself feel better. Or perhaps, you think if you yell at him he will never forget to take it out again. Or maybe, you are frustrated with him for other reasons and the trash incident was just a chance to express some built up frustration. Being mindful of your true intent can lead to more effective ways of handling situations or shed light on issues you have been trying to bury.

In addition to observing your intent after an action, be mindful of your intent before you speak or act today. Ask yourself "What is my intention?" before making any decision. This can be as simple as deciding where to eat for lunch or an email you are sending to a coworker. This approach will often lead to more effective decision-making and interactions with others.

DAY 6: Mindful Awareness

True self-awareness is a result of constant mindfulness. Through time, we have formed many habits that affect our natural inclinations, how we think, act, and perceive the world. Have you ever stepped back and really observed how you navigate the world?

Today is your chance to break habituated patterns and discover natural tendencies. Focus on your routines, thinking patterns, conversation patterns, natural tendencies, and general outlook on life. Also, be mindful of the results your natural tendencies encourage. As with all the mindful activities, just observe. You can always work to shift certain patterns later, but you must be fully aware of them first.

DAY 7: Mindful Gratitude

Expressing gratitude has been shown to drastically decrease stress, anxiety and a variety of other negative emotions. When we express gratitude we focus on what we have to be grateful for in our lives. This practice, combined with mindfulness, can drastically shift one's outlook.

For today, be mindful of everything you have to be grateful for. Often, our minds want to focus on negatives, especially in moments of agitation, but there is always something to be grateful for. Perhaps, be mindful that your heart and lungs are working efficiently, or you have full control over all of your limbs, or you are surrounded by people you love.

Throughout the day, bring mindful attention to what you are grateful for in each moment. Any time you experience a negative emotion, anger, frustration, guilt, anxiety, overwhelm, etc. refocus your mind to what you are grateful for in that moment and watch how this impacts the negative emotion.

30 DAY Mindfulness Challenge Week Four

This week you will focus on being mindful for periods of time throughout your day. You have already practiced being mindful in particular tasks and you are now ready to extend this to a few hours at a time.

Like the initial two weeks, you will start with a 'Mindful Day'. This is meant to gauge your progress, so remember not to judge or try to change anything but just observe yourself.

Feel free to continue mindful meditation practices, even though they are not specifically stated in the daily challenges. It is encouraged to engage in 5-20 minutes of mindful meditation in addition to the daily exercises.

This is your final week of the challenge. Give yourself credit for all the hard work so far and good luck!

DAY 1: Mindful Day

It is the final week and the perfect time to observe your progress. Today, just be mindful of how you navigate the world. Pay attention to what you think, feel, and how you act and respond to situations. The goal is to be as mindful as you can without any judgment or trying to change anything.

Notice times or tasks in which you are more or less mindful. This Mindful Day will be like falling in and out of a dream. You will be mindful for a while and then will slip back into your own non-mindful state. Once you realized you slipped back into this "dream" state, simply bring your attention back to the present.

DAY 2: Mindful Morning

Focus on being mindful from the time you wake up until midday. Set an end time for yourself around noon and aim to be mindful for the entire chunk of time.

Your mind will stray, but when you notice it does, simply bring yourself back to the present. Be mindful during any relaxing, walking, commuting, conversations, morning tasks, thoughts that arise, and anytime you experience emotions.

You are equipped to be mindful in all these situations; it is simply time to put them together and practice. After the morning is over, reflect on how it went for you. Did you struggle during a particular time, with certain situations or tasks? Try to figure out what happened during those times that led you to become unmindful. Once you are aware of challenges, you are able to be extra mindful during these situations in the future. Don't worry, you will have time again tomorrow to practice this exercise.

DAY 3: Mindful Afternoon

Just as yesterday, you are going to be mindful in every task during a chunk of time. Pick the time you stopped the exercise yesterday as a beginning point. It may even be helpful to set an alarm for yourself so you do not forget. Also, pick an end time in the early evening (between 4-7 o'clock) to finish the exercise.

Your mind will inevitably wander during this time, and when you notice it does, simply bring yourself back to the present. Be mindful during any relaxing, walking, eating, commuting, conversations, afternoon tasks, thoughts that arise, and anytime you experience emotions. You are equipped to be mindful in all these situations; it is simply time to put them together and practice.

Notice if this time period is easier or harder than the morning. Often, we become tired in the afternoon, which may benefit or hinder your mindful attempt. You may also observe times that are challenging, such as after a meeting or during your evening commute. Be aware of what makes certain situations or times harder to remain mindful. It can provide invaluable insight into thinking patterns and sources of stress in your life.

DAY 4: Mindful Evening

Just as you have done the previous two days, you will be mindful for a pre-determined period of time. Whatever time you stopped your mindful exercise yesterday, begin at that time today. Remain mindful for the entire evening. End the exercise before bed as that will be the focus tomorrow.

Make sure you are mindful during eating, relaxing, all tasks, preparations for the next day, and during all conversations. Try to only engage in tasks that will make it easy to be mindful. For example, watching mindless TV or searching the web are situations that make it challenging to stay mindful. Instead, think of activities such as exercise, an artistic endeavor, or even meditation you can engage in to relax and remain present.

DAY 5: Mindful Bedtime and Sleep Prep

As the final stage of the day-long mindfulness practice, you are going to focus on being mindful right before sleep. During this period, people like to replay all the events of the day, think about stressful situations in their lives, and plan and/or worry about everything they need to get done the following day. This is not beneficial and can be very detrimental to your sleep quantity and quality.

It may be helpful to journal in the evening before you practice mindfulness, especially if bedtime is something you struggle with. You can write down a to-do list for the next day or write anything you need to get out your mind about present or past situations. This is not part of the mindful practice but fosters a beneficial mental state for mindfulness.

The instant you get into bed, only focus on sensations during each present moment. Feel the pressure of your body against the mattress and feel the covers touching different areas of your body. Focus on the temperature of your body and if any parts are warmer or cooler. Focus on how your body feels and if parts are tense or relaxed. Focus on your breathing and how the breath feels entering and exiting your lungs. Focus on any sounds and smells.

Remember not to place a single judgment on anything you observe. If your partner is listening to TV loudly in the other room, do not say the TV is loud, but simply note it is a sound and move on to other sensations. The less you allow thinking and judgments to enter your mind, the less likely you are to spin into a state of negativity or anxiousness, which prevents you from falling asleep.

Note the feelings as you become more tired and allow yourself to drift off naturally. If you fall asleep one minute after lying down, great! Do not feel pressure to stay up just to be mindful, but be mindful for as long as you are awake. If you struggle, pick a mindful meditation that worked well for you and go through it to calm your mind and body in preparation for sleep.

DAY 6: Not Thinking About the Past

There is peace in the present. The past does not affect you unless you remember it and associate feelings with it. The past is simply a moment in time. Today, practice living in the moment and not thinking about the past.

Notice anytime a thought of a past experience enters your mind. This can be a situation, a person, a conversation, or a moment. Do not continue to think about or pair any emotion with this thought, good or bad. Just let it pass out of your mind as easily as it came in. If it tries to come in again, let it go again. Do not put any more energy into it other than noticing it is a thought passing through. As soon as the thought passes, be extra mindful in that moment. What are you doing? Draw from all of the exercises to practice this mindfulness.

Remember the past is any moment that has passed. It can be 10 years ago or 10 minutes ago. Today, you will aim not to think about anything that has passed. If you have a conversation with a parent on the phone, as soon as the conversation is over, you will not think about what was said. That moment has passed. Simply focus attention on the current moment. If you just heard a hilarious joke, do not think about that joke afterward. Not reminiscing about positive events may seem counterproductive, but anytime you think of something from the past you are not being mindful.

For today, do not focus on anything that comes up about any passed event, good or bad, near or far, and just stay present. Say it now: *Today I will not think about any past event, good or bad, and will only focus on each present moment.*

DAY 7: Not Thinking About the Future

Today will be similar to yesterday, but opposite! Today you will not allow yourself to think of the future. What?!! This sounds crazy! How will you ever get anything done??

Yes, this may be the most anxiety-provoking activity so far, if you let it. Ideally, mindfulness is the consistent practice of being in the present moment which means there is no thought about the future. However, with work and responsibilities, it can be almost impossible to live in such a manner.

For this exercise, feel free to engage in a modified version true mindfulness. Make a schedule for the day and/or plan out what needs to be done for work or any other responsibilities. Other than this brief planning, do not think about anything besides what you are doing at that moment. If you are answering emails, focus only on what you are writing at the time and not what you need to do after you send the email. If you are eating lunch, enjoy your lunch and do not think about what you need to do after you finish. If you are driving your children to an activity, be fully present in that experience instead of thinking about what you have to do after you drop them off.

This will likely be very challenging at moments, but by now you are fully equipped to handle it. When you notice your thoughts drifting to the future, near or far, let them drift out of your mind and refocus yourself in the present situation. Draw from any practices you learned during this challenge to help you do this. You will likely find everything you need to get done, gets done, and with a lot less stress and drained energy.

If you need to take a few moments in your day to re-plan, that's
okay. Just be sure to engage in every present moment fully instead
of thinking about what is next.

Bonus Day Challenge: The Mindful Day

This is a time when you put together all of the practices and knowledge you have learned.

Wake up mindful

Morning Mindfulness

10-minute Mindfulness Meditation

Mindful Eating Breakfast

Mindful Driving, Commuting, and Walking all day

Mindful Conversations all day

Mindful Afternoon

Mindful Eating Lunch

No Thinking about The Past or Future entire day

Mindful Driving, Walking, Commuting

Mindful Activities

Mindful Relaxing

Mindful Observations

Mindful Evening

Mindful Bedtime and Sleep Prep

You can do this!
It is time to really test how far you have come.

Conclusion

Congratulations on making it through the challenge! It is not easy to commit yourself to such a journey. You have now established a strong mindfulness base and with continued practice, you will regain control of your thinking, emotions, and your life.

Situations that once frustrated you will no longer seem important. You will be able to savor life's precious moments and be peaceful in almost any situation. Mindfulness will also help you face obstacles and challenges without becoming overwhelmed. By staying mindful through all situations, good, bad, and indifferent, you are able to remain centered and calm no matter what is happening in your world.

Others will notice the change as well. Family and friends appreciate the undivided attention and you may also encourage others to be more present-focused. The calm energy you give off will become contagious, affecting everyone you come in contact with.

You will also find you get far more accomplished. A lot of time is wasted on indecisiveness. Mindfulness creates a clear mental environment that facilitates ease of decision-making. Also, by only focusing on one task at a time, you will accomplish tasks quicker and more efficiently.

Trust the mindful process. Know it takes practice and your ingrained habits and thinking patterns will try to coerce you back into old, comfortable patterns. With effort, practice, and commitment, you will begin to live the blissful life we all desire.

First Book in the Mindfulness Series, ***Beginners Guide to Mindfulness in a World of Chaos***, is available **on Amazon!**

Second Book in Mindfulness Series, ***Mindful Mornings: Daily Reflections and Meditations,*** is available **on Amazon!**

out a contract or any guarantee assurance.

The trademarks that are used are without any consent, and the publication of the trademark is without permission or backing by the trademark owner. All trademarks and brands within this book are for clarifying purposes only and are the owned by the owners themselves, not affiliated with this document.